The Life and Undeath of Autonomy
in American Literature

The Life and Undeath of Autonomy in American Literature

GEOFF HAMILTON

University of Virginia Press

CHARLOTTESVILLE AND LONDON

University of Virginia Press

Printed in the United States of America on acid-free paper

First published 2014

9 8 7 6 5 4 3 2 1

LIBRARY OF CONGRESS CATALOGING-IN-PUBLICATION DATA

Hamilton, Geoff, [date]
  The life and undeath of autonomy in American literature / Geoff Hamilton.
    pages cm
  Includes bibliographical references and index.
  ISBN 978-0-8139-3528-7 (cloth : alk. pbk.)
  ISBN 978-0-8139-3529-4 (pbk. : alk. pbk.)
  ISBN 978-0-8139-3530-0 (e-book)
  1. American literature—History and criticism. 2. Self in literature. 3. Autonomy in literature. 4. Persona (Literature). I. Title.
PS169.S425H36 2014
810.9'353—dc23

                                                          2013013896

THE AMERICAN LITERATURES INITIATIVE

A book in the American Literatures Initiative (ALI), a collaborative publishing project of NYU Press, Fordham University Press, Rutgers University Press, Temple University Press, and the University of Virginia Press. The Initiative is supported by The Andrew W. Mellon Foundation. For more information, please visit www.americanliteratures.org.

For my parents, Henry and Beryl

Nothing is at last sacred but the integrity of your own mind. Absolve you to yourself, and you shall have the suffrage of the world. I remember an answer which when quite young I was prompted to make to a valued adviser who was wont to importune me with the dear old doctrines of the church. On my saying, "What have I to do with the sacredness of traditions, if I live wholly from within?" my friend suggested,—"But these impulses may be from below, not from above." I replied, "They do not seem to me to be such; but if I am the Devil's child, I will live then from the Devil." No law can be sacred to me but that of my nature.

—EMERSON, "SELF-RELIANCE"

Contents

Acknowledgments

This book is about autonomy, but I was anything but wholly self-lawed or self-inhabited in writing it. I wish to thank, above all, Tom Adamowski, Andre Furlani, and Brian Jones for their invaluable help in shepherding a wide and sometimes unruly pasture.

The Life and Undeath of Autonomy
in American Literature

Introduction

From the founding of America to the contemporary moment, conceptions of autonomy have been central to the nation's political and imaginative life. Given that centrality, and the fact that both the "self" (auto) in auto-nomy, and the social "order" (*nomos*) in which it is expressed, have changed dramatically over the course of American history, it is remarkable that critical discussions of the concept so often treat it statically and ahistorically, ignoring its complex evolution, which began long before there ever was an America, or even a New World.

The Life and Undeath of Autonomy charts this evolution. Though its structural focus lies on the writings of major authors in the American canon, its overarching narrative describes a sequence of startling and profound changes unfolding in the heart of the national imaginary, respecting not only autonomy, but a host of affiliated themes with both "literary" and sociopolitical dimensions, including the place of the divine in personal and political life, the strength of communal allegiances, the dominion of the "laws of nature," the role of violence in identity formation, and the fate of autonomy's conceptual kin—"liberty," "freedom," and "the pursuit of happiness." In addition, the study's evolutionary narrative—which limits itself to the work (and, largely, the experience) of white males—will, I hope, set a broad conceptual stage for exploring the equally if not more important narrative that runs alongside and against this one, namely, the *search* for autonomy in works by women and nonwhite authors.

Charting autonomy's evolution over the span of American literary history, and against a classical analogue, can add invaluable "depth perception," I suggest, to our understanding of the concept. Consider, for instance, the wording of the Declaration itself. Though scholars now routinely speak of autonomy in political and human terms—debating such topics as the rights of autonomous peoples, or the autonomous decision-making of rational individuals—America's inaugural claim to an autonomous or self-lawed existence in fact appealed to the *opposites* of these terms, the pastoral and the divine. The "one people" of the United States announced their right to rule themselves, as Thomas Jefferson phrased it, so that they might "assume among the powers of the earth, the separate and equal station to which the Laws of Nature and of Nature's God entitle them" ("Declaration" 19). In *Notes on the State of Virginia* (1784), Jefferson elaborated on his vision of the ideal American life, describing a utopia governed by natural law and divinely blessed through its proximity to the natural world: "Those who labour in the earth," he affirmed, "are the chosen people of God, if ever he had a chosen people, whose breasts he has made his peculiar deposit for substantial and genuine virtue" (290).

Nor, of course, was Jefferson's vision historically unique. In fact, we find a telling prefiguration of his "Nature's God" in the ancient Greeks' Themis, and of his "Laws of Nature" in her daughter Eunomia. Themis (as in our "theme," something "set and fixed") was the goddess of divine, unwritten law (*themis*). Eunomia ("Good Pasture/Order/Law"), a quintessential pastoral power, was worshipped by farmers dependent upon the progress of the seasons, and gave meaning to agricultural life according to a fusion of natural and human law. Writing in the sixth century BCE, Solon reminds his fellow citizens of Eunomia's role, while cautioning them about her dark opposite: "This I am compelled to teach Athenians, that Dysnomia [Bad Pasture/Order/Law] brings the city numberless ills, but Eunomia reveals all that is orderly and right, and often restrains the unjust. She makes rough things smooth, limits excess, reduces hubris, sterilizes the flowering of destruction, straightens crooked judgments, tames acts of pride, and ends sedition and the wrath of calamitous strife" (Solon, Fragment 4).[1] That *eunomic* fusion of the pastoral and the political was obscured by the rise of the ancient (and modern) polis, but dramatically reborn—as the stage on which the nation's own claim to self-rule (auto-nomy) would be performed—in the American arcadia.

As we track autonomy's evolution, and consider affinities between American and Greek literary characters—Natty Bumppo and Odysseus,

Emerson's "poet" and Socrates, Cormac McCarthy's Judge Holden and Callicles, et al.—we may see more clearly not merely what American literary history has in common with that of ancient Greece, but what is distinctively its own. Both Greek and American literature chronicle, for instance, the gradual separation of human and divine law, followed by the rise of nomistic detachment and private claims to *themis*. American autonomy, however, dramatically surpasses its Greek counterpart in the expression of self-law, and its literary history reveals the emergence of a set of quintessentially American features: most critically, an emphasis on radical self-renewal (severing the self from history) and egalitarianism (autonomy as universally available), an idealization of solitary predation according to the "laws of nature" (associated with so-called "regenerative violence"), and at last a profound implication in technological prosthetics (as the means to make and remake the self). Moreover, a long view of literary history helps us perceive the critical stages of autonomy's evolution in American literature itself—from its early, optimistic formulations, to its pathologies in the twentieth and twenty-first centuries—along with the various ways in which authors from later literary eras revise past conceptions of autonomy: for instance, the Transcendentalists' elaboration of Jeffersonian pastoralism and augmented insistence on the self's private communion with the divine, or Gary Shteyngart's "posthuman" reconstruction, in the age of social networking, of Whitman's self-celebrations.

Examining representative works of American literature in relation to those of ancient Greece might also add a complementary, literary perspective to recent studies by social and political historians which trace the influence of classicism—typically filtered through the European Enlightenment—on the American imaginary.[2] "Old myths," as Carl J. Richard puts it in his study of the Founders' classical debts, "became the essential catalysts for the production of new realities" (Richard 9):

> Although the Greeks and Romans had emphasized civic duties over individual rights, they had also acknowledged the right of society to be free from arbitrary government, an idea revolutionary for its day and fraught with (then unpursued) implications for the individual. The founders viewed the American experience (including their own experiences) through the same classically based prism. Free from the stain of feudalism and possessed of abundant land, American society was uniquely capable of translating classical ideals into reality. (9)

Though America's imaginative kinship with the ancient world forms the context in which this study takes place, my interest is not in examining the specific ways in which the old was borrowed and made new. Rather than tracking direct conceptual borrowings, or teasing out the complexities of influence at particular historical moments, what I seek to chart here are conceptual affinities (and differences) between two strikingly similar imaginative histories. As I hope to illustrate, we find in both archaic Greece and early America a mythopoeic fusion of human and natural worlds—a *eunomia* which gradually dissolves, in roughly analogous ways, with the growth of autonomy.

The rich and evocative etymology of the word "autonomy" itself forms part of the critical vocabulary employed by this study: the ancient Greek noun *autonomia* combines *auto-*, "self," with *–nomos*, whose root snakes down from our "custom," "convention," "rule," or "law" (*nomos*), to the critical archaic Greek gesture of *nemo*, which Homer frequently employed, in reference to food and drink, to mean "deal out, dispense, order, or assign." *Nemo* was, however, associated in other, more complex ways with the management of earthly sustenance; it can mean "to pasture or tend flocks" in a *nomos* (as "pasture"), "to feed upon or graze" (in the Greek "middle" sense of self-reference), "to have to oneself or possess," "to inhabit," and, metaphorically, "to consume (in a fire)" and "to spread (like an ulcer)." *Autonomia* thus presents a vivid semantic palette, imbuing the auto-nomy that figures so prominently in the American imaginary with root-shades of "self-pasture," "self-possession," "self-inhabitance," "self-consumption," and even, should the self itself become pasture, "self-destruction."[3]

This study begins with a brief consideration of the birth and roots of autonomy in ancient Greece, then uses this heuristic backdrop to examine the development of autonomy (self-law/self-pasture) in American literature through its most critical stages, from the Declaration to the contemporary moment. My focus, I should emphasize, does not lie on the actual use made (or not made) of classical texts and ideas by selected American authors; nor am I concerned with analyzing these authors' various deployments of the actual word "autonomy," or with accounting for the way they revised their ideas over time. Rather, my interest here is in observing, using a classical precedent and representative examples of crucial moments in American literature, the "life cycle" of autonomy in literary representations. Nor, I should stress, do I wish any teleological or deterministic sense to be ascribed to my strictly *narrative* use of such terms as "life cycle" or "stages" in telling the story of autonomy in my chosen authors. What I seek to provide here is a retrospective account of what actually happened to the concept, not what had to happen.

My hope, most broadly, is to demonstrate the way in which such representations chart a profound transition in the sense of self-pasture, from a nourishing liberty of fulfillment (as in Jeffersonian pastoralism and, more extremely, Transcendentalism and the mythology of the frontiersman), through an aggressive, atomizing agency destructive to both human and natural worlds (as exemplified in McCarthy's *Blood Meridian*), to a final pasturing *on* the self, its ultimate *hyper*autonomy or "undeath," involving a spiraling inwardness, sterile isolation, and, in a culminating inversion of the detachment marking autonomy's most positive stages, a radical receptivity to nomistic powers (as in selected works by Don DeLillo and Shteyngart). This approach certainly implies a good deal about the role played by various historical realities (for instance, the closing of the frontier, the growth of industrialization and urbanization, the rise of the mass media, etc.), but it has as its primary objective the exploration of conceptual change itself.

Two critical weaknesses, intimated above, seem apparent in extant studies of autonomy in the American imaginary. The first is a tendency to approach the subject statically, often in terms of relatively brief historical spans, and thus severely limit (and, I would argue, distort) any sense of its dynamic, evolutionary features. Though the concept of autonomy has its roots in the beginnings of Western civilization, it has been conventional to speak of America's experiment in self-law primarily in relation to seventeenth- and eighteenth-century intellectual movements. Many of the most influential studies of American autonomy (or "individualism," of which more anon)—such as R. W. B. Lewis's *The American Adam: Innocence, Tragedy, and Tradition in the Nineteenth Century* (1955), Quentin Anderson's *The Imperial Self: An Essay in American Literary and Cultural History* (1971), Myra Jehlen's *American Incarnation: The Individual, The Nation, and the Continent* (1986), Mark R. Patterson's *Authority, Autonomy, and Representation in American Literature, 1776–1865*, and Richard Slotkin's trilogy—*Regeneration through Violence: The Mythology of the American Frontier 1600–1860* (1973), *The Fatal Environment: The Myth of the Frontier in the Age of Industrialization 1800–1890* (1985), *Gunfighter Nation: The Myth of the Frontier in Twentieth-Century America* (1992)—focus solely on limited periods of the modern era. In addition, these studies, given their publication dates, have little or nothing to say about the last several decades of American literature.

Jehlen's seminal *American Incarnation*, which assesses what she calls "the culminating evolution of individualism" (Jehlen vii), seems to underscore the lacuna noted above. In briefly referring to ancient figures such as Odysseus, Oedipus, and Antigone, she points to *disjunctions* between ancient and modern constructions of the self, and identifies "this country's originating ideas" as "derived from the essential principles of the European Reformation and Enlightenment" (3). In contrast, I am primarily interested in tracing *conjunctions* between ancient and modern worlds, and in highlighting parallels between them rather than specific intellectual derivations (though the latter are, of course, plentiful, as I note in my chapter on Jefferson). What Jehlen dubs "the American incarnation," a fusion of the self with the land and the nation that produced "a civilization that is [understood to be] the human dimension of nature" (59), I examine here under the rubric of *eunomia* and in terms of affinities between American representations of autonomy and their Greek precedent—an examination that extends through the twentieth century and up to the present moment.

More recent studies that explore the destructive aspects of self-law in contemporary fiction (as well as other cultural products), such as Mark Seltzer's *Serial Killers: Death and Life in America's Wound Culture* (1998), Philip L. Simpson's *Psycho Paths: Tracing the Serial Killer through Contemporary American Film and Fiction* (2000), Marilyn C. Wesley's *Violent Adventure: Contemporary Fiction by American Men* (2003), or David Schmid's *Natural Born Celebrities: Serial Killers in American Culture* (2005), also limit their consideration of autonomy to American literature, and to a span of, at most, the last hundred or so years. What Seltzer calls, for instance, the "mass in person," the "uniform and uniformed individual and the standardized personation of the social law" (Seltzer 160), a kind of black hole of selfhood, void but feeding endlessly upon the world around it, is understood in my own work against the backdrop of classical autonomy and in relation to its crucial developmental stages in American literature. In order to understand the "uncertain boundaries between self and society" which form our "pathological public sphere" or "wound culture" (137), it seems useful to add this kind of "depth perception" to our consideration of American selves and the nomistic worlds they inhabit.

To take a specific example—elaborated on in my chapters on the Transcendentalists and the contemporary novelists DeLillo and Shteyngart—we might note the connection between the hyperpermeable selfhood of

Seltzer's "mass in person" and its inversion of (perhaps most obviously) Walt Whitman's optimistic project of identification with the masses in the nineteenth century. In *this* study, the serial killer's "dream of a direct filiation with Nature," "of a direct *fusion* with an indistinct mass of others" (19; italics in original) is theorized not only in relation to earlier, developmental stages in American literature (including the Transcendentalists' absorptive selfhood and the frontiersman's predatory aggression), but to the imaginative history of autonomy in a compelling classical precedent. With such an approach, the serial killer's pathological "direct filiation with Nature" can be seen not only as a culminating phenomenon in America's experiment in eunomic autonomy—amounting to a sensational negation of Whitman's optimism about self-law within mass culture—but as an extreme, modern analogue to the rise of autonomy and the dissolution of *eunomia* in ancient Greece.

A second weakness of extant works in this area, it seems to me, lies in their tendency to employ tractable but insubstantial conceptual surrogates for the rich but demanding concept of autonomy. For example, philosophers as well as literary scholars often use "individualism" and "autonomy" (or "individual autonomy," to distinguish it from corporate entities, such as "state autonomy") interchangeably. "Individualism," however, is simply the ism of a negation, the quality of being undivided, a single, atomic thing. The noun "individual" comes to English from the medieval Latin—*individuus*—something "indivisible, inseparable"—and took on the senses relevant here between the fifteenth and seventeenth centuries in the context of feudal society's decline: "One in substance or essence; forming an indivisible entity; indivisible," "Single, as distinct from others of the same kind; particular, special," "Distinguished from others by attributes of its own; marked by a peculiar and striking character," "Of, pertaining or peculiar to, a single person or thing, or some one member of a class; characteristic of an individual," "A single human being, as opposed to Society, the Family, etc." (*OED*). Though "individualism" is conventionally used to imply the liberty of self-law, and since Tocqueville's *Democracy in America* (1835, 1840) has been strongly associated with American national character, the term itself suggests merely an atomic quality—the practice or principle of being separate, set apart from, and not subsumed within, a larger class of things (such as, for instance, a feudal identity and network of social obligations). Moreover, "individualism" began to lose whatever descriptive relevance it had not long after it was coined in the early nineteenth century, since "individuals," at least since Freud, have been thought of as *fundamentally* divided, a multitude of things (and anything *but* autonomous, even in their dreams). Nevertheless, critics' definitions of "individual" sometimes include the word "autonomous," and thereby project onto the former term's "blankness" a substantive element that more properly belongs to the other, much richer and older term. Cyrus R. K. Patell provides a representative example of this semantic maneuver in his *Negative Liberties: Morrison, Pynchon, and the Problem of Liberal Ideology* (2001): "The champions of negative liberty attend first and foremost to the claims of the individual; they are interested in the ways in which the individual may be said to *be* individual—to be a single, indivisible, autonomous agent and a possessor of rights" (Patell 18; italics in original). An "individual" is single and indivisible, but not *necessarily* an "autonomous agent and a possessor of rights." The definition provided by Robert N. Bellah et al., in one of the prefaces to *Habits of the Heart: Individualism and Commitment in American Life* (1985, 1996, 2008), performs a similar act of conceptual supererogation, attributing to "individualism" a characteristic ("self-reliance") that more fittingly belongs, I suggest, to "autonomy": "Individualism, the first language in which Americans tend to think about their lives, values independence and self-reliance above all else" (Bellah et al. xiv).

This study favors the term "autonomy" over "individualism," but continues to use "individual" to indicate a single self when what is implied is simply the separation of that self from a collective entity (as in, say, discussions of an individual's conflict with her community). However, I have chosen to use "*personal* autonomy" and "autonomous *person*," rather than the more familiar "individual autonomy" and "autonomous individual," since the former pair seem more accurate and suggestive in conveying the characteristics of self-law. Derived from the Latin *persona* ("a mask"), and linked to ancient theater, the English noun "person" can mean both "a role" and "a human being" (*OED*). Unlike "individual," "person" is associated with a specific action—the adoption of a mask, the assumption of a role. The literary history of personal autonomy in the American imaginary demonstrates, furthermore, how personae proliferate as the range of self-law grows, and therefore implies the value of a term which brings to mind the power of self-construction (the making of roles). This value should become most obvious later in the study as I examine hyperautonomy, the culminating stage in the growth of self-law. Here, personal autonomy has grown so powerful that it begins to evoke the ancient sense of "person" as *merely* a mask—or more precisely, a dizzying plurality of technologically mediated roles that are, seemingly, estranged from any stable sense of a single "human being," and not at all "individual."

The less than two-hundred-year history of "individualism" gives us further reason to prefer its alternative. Applying the word to early American literature and the foundational mythology expressed there is obviously anachronistic, and makes it easier to imply that articulations of America's special relationship to self-law have nothing in common with ideas originating more than a few centuries before the Revolution. Using "individualism" in fact helps to obscure what is most similar (or interestingly dissimilar) about analogous literary histories, including the stages in which *eunomia* dissolves with the growth of autonomy, and the manner in which the *American* version of that process exceeds the dimensions of its Greek precedent and takes on distinctive features of its own. Literary accounts of "individualism," therefore, seem ready to benefit from some conceptual clarification.

Autonomy, in contrast, carries with it a tremendous historical and semantic richness. The word has a 2,500-year history, beginning with its first extant deployment, in adjectival form, during a crucial moment in *Antigone* (440 BCE). It is, furthermore, a substantive term, whose substance—most basically, "self-law"—is easily visible in the word itself. This substance is the core of what scholars typically, but not invariably, want to indicate with "individualism"—that is, the notion of existing under one's own control and not someone else's, of heeding one's own authority, having and exercising liberty, being free. The inadequacy of "individualism" as a means of describing her central topic, the ideology of American identification with the land, seems clear in the following passage from Jehlen's *American Incarnation*: "This concept of America, as a natural world animate with human purpose, was an extraordinary vision, projecting an individualism that, for being lord of its own global acres, was literally universal, at the heart of everything that happened everywhere" (Jehlen 74). Replacing "individualism" with "autonomy" in this passage dramatically enhances its precision and associative power, for the latter conveys exactly the sense of command, of independent power and unlimited range, of "lordship" rather than atomic blankness, that is at issue in Jehlen's analysis.

As noted above, the etymology of "autonomy" (with root shades suggesting the linking of "self" with "pasture," "possession," "inhabitance," "consumption," and "destruction [as ulcer or fire]") only enriches the word's relationship to the concept of self-law—again, in contrast to the blank quality of "individualism." Consider now the following sentence from Patell's *Negative Liberties*: "[Rugged] individualism, the myth of the heroic loner embodied by the frontiersman and the cowboy, is linked historically to an acquisitive hunger for dominion over both lands and peoples, a desire to domesticate the American continent by dividing it into parcels owned by individuals" (Patell 29–30). If we substitute "autonomy" for "individualism" above, the statement gains remarkable new resonance and theoretical profundity. In this articulation, the mythology of the American frontier is set against the backdrop of its Greek precedent—provoking a range of associative links—and can, in addition, be seen to fulfill several originary senses of *autonomia*. The mythology of "rugged autonomy," we may note, both repeats and hyperbolizes the terms of an ancient analogue: the frontiersman and the cowboy, feeding upon the New World, sought to inhabit and possess the land for themselves, and spread—at least from the perspective of prior inhabitants who encountered these figures' "acquisitive hunger for dominion over both lands and peoples"—like an ulcer, fierily consuming the parcels of territory divided between them.

It remains to make clear what this work can and cannot hope to do, beyond the aims stated above, especially in the face of two very important related areas which it borders and, therefore, partly frames. The first concerns the significance of autonomy, and of the particular narrative of autonomy described by my work, in the literature (and experience) of women and nonwhite writers. The second, which clearly intersects with the first, concerns the significance of that limited narrative to the wider contemporary context of sociopolitical debate in America.[4] The first really comprises two (and more) distinct narratives of its own, which follow along beside, and interact with, the (essentially white male) narrative I am describing, from the earliest years of the European colonies in America. These have dramatically different, even opposite narrative trajectories, and are still very much in the ascendance today, while mine, I argue, has peaked and declined to a strange sort of conceptual undeath. The second begins, in a sense, where my literary narrative ends, stretching out in a series of now problematized conceptual vectors, from the complex conceptual nexus described in the late stages of my story.

These two related areas are far too important, rich, and complex to be addressed substantively in the confines of what must, to some, seem an already much too ambitious study. However, my hope is that, in outlining the essential contours of its chosen narrative, the work might lay some useful conceptual groundwork for extensive studies running parallel to and beyond its borders. That is, by articulating the "positive" narrative space of autonomy in its chosen authors, it might helpfully limn the "negative" space beyond it, for future study and dialogue.

As that second negative space—the sociopolitical implications of my narrative of autonomy—is principally defined by the late-stage contours of the narrative, it seemed best, beyond the ongoing *implicit* characterization of the space in the later chapters of the book, to briefly but explicitly address it at the conclusion of the work. But what, I wondered, could possibly be said, briefly but not absurdly, about that first negative space: vast, multifaceted, and effectively coextensive with the limited narrative of the book?

Encouragingly, I realized that indeed a great deal *is* being said about it, throughout the narrative, implicitly and, as it were, "negatively," in the way that the positive space in a sculpture is speaking of and to the negative. To anyone even casually familiar with the rise, hegemony, and late-twentieth-century crisis of white male Eurocentric culture in America, the narrative will serve as a constant reminder of the antithetical Other struggling, suffering, waiting, and working—at the borders of this narrative—for a real and enduring measure of the autonomy largely taken for granted by that culture.

To those with some familiarity with the voices of that Other, the narrative will, I hope, offer a conceptual stage on which those voices can profitably speak, a point to their counterpoint—and, as I suggested earlier, perhaps stage in its turn a future study, or studies, exploring at a length and depth befitting the magnitude and profundity of their experience, the (still ongoing) rise of meaningful autonomy. The importantly different historical and literary trajectories of African Americans, Native Americans, women, and others denied self-rule from Jefferson on down, expose the profoundly unequal distribution and fulfillment of the promises articulated in the Declaration or *Notes on the State of Virginia*. These trajectories suggest nothing like a gradual transition from enormous potential power to a paradoxical undeath, but instead a tragically late and hard-won, but increasingly vigorous *life*, in stark contrast to the literature and experience of the subjects explored in this study. To take one example, Louise Erdrich's poem "Dear John Wayne"—published just one year before Cormac McCarthy's *Blood Meridian* explored the conditions of (white American) autonomy's sublime meridian and the advent of its lingering undeath—offers a vigorous assertion of Native Americans' long-denied right to autonomy, and posits such a claim as necessarily waged against the genocidal legacy of white hegemony. Such trajectories, of early and often brutal oppression, but then increasing and increasingly enduring empowerment, enfranchisement, racial and gender equality, and autonomous life, are virtually mirror opposites of the one explored here; while the critical concepts allied to autonomy, such as authority and authenticity, or the relationship between the human *nomos* and divine *themis*, typically have opposite valencies for the oppressor and oppressed. The complex interplay between these opposite valencies, and those opposite trajectories, deserves nothing less, it seems to me, than a major work of its own.

Chapter 1, in tracing the emergence of autonomy in ancient Greece, looks at the complex shades within *nomos* itself, beginning with an exploration of its mythopoeic roots in the primal eunomic fusion of the pastoral and political and then charting its dissolution with the rise of the polis and its *human* (versus divine) *nomos*, which is now contrasted to *themis*. My first examples come from Homer, where I consider the potency of *themis* as a limit to human authority and ambition, as well as the portents of its decline. Particularly remarkable here is Odysseus's profound ironic detachment from the nomistic world, which uncannily anticipates, I suggest, the contemporary "psychopathic type." Next I turn to Sophocles's *Antigone*—which contains the earliest extant deployment of the specific concept of autonomy in Western literature— and its commentary on the social threat posed by personal autonomy. I then consider the character Callicles in Plato's *Gorgias* and his defense of *physis*, the "law of nature" that ostensibly sets all humans against one another in pitiless competition; Callicles is, I will argue, analogous to later proponents of a brutal "naturalism" in American literature, such as McCarthy's Judge Holden. I turn next to Plato's Socrates and the actual *valorization* of the autonomous person. To his highly political culture, Socrates was a threatening *idiotes* ("private man"), self-possessed and self-shepherding within the Athenian *nomos*, an elenchic examiner of all conventional opinion, yet steadfastly obedient to a now reduced but enduring themistic presence. Finally, I note an even more extreme stage of eunomic dissolution in Epicurus, who professes the importance of asocial happiness, thoroughly separate from the nomistic sphere. Odysseus, Callicles, Antigone, Socrates, and Epicurus will be recalled, as the study progresses, in juxtaposition with the various American permutations of autonomy.

In chapter 2, I turn to Jefferson and the modern age, where *eunomia* is reborn in the American arcadia, but now in a form that sponsors a more wide-ranging, egalitarian, and indeed explosive kind of autonomy, whose dangers remain, for the most part, only latent in its early stages. Jefferson's fundamental conviction is that the looser force of government under the American republic will not create anarchy but instead foster— and indeed harmonize—personal and corporate virtue. His America would, of course, retain a sturdy nomistic structure, but one that would essentially reconstitute the Greeks' sense of *nomos* as nourished by *themis*, the people's moral life and destiny framed by a supernal—and "natural"—order (Themis, we may recall, is the mother of Eunomia). However, in the young republic, themistic authority would be placed beyond the claim of any human ruler. Here one could pursue a political and religious life as one could not in Europe, free of monarchical shepherds, part of an independent, rational, and educated citizenry, self-lawed in self-pasture. The American flock would, as it were, shepherd itself, relying upon its common, divinely suffused *nomos* for guidance. Though Jefferson's stress clearly falls on autonomy in its corporate dimension, his optimistic endorsement of reduced human governance, and his own dedication to skeptical inquiry, prepare the way for the more extreme notions of personal autonomy articulated by the Transcendentalists, as well as its ultimate development in the pathological pasturage of hyperautonomy. I conclude this chapter by looking briefly at Charles Brockden Brown's novel *Wieland* (1798)[5] and its description of a gentleman farmer who, calamitously breaking away from the nomistic world as he claims a wholly *private* access to *themis*, slaughters his family. This Gothic tale emphasizes autonomy's lurking (but still nascent) explosiveness, and casts a shadow over Jefferson's pastoralism in a proleptic figuration of self-pasture's late-stage complications.

The mythic frontiersman and the origins of what D. H. Lawrence memorably described as the "essential American soul," the New World man who is "hard, isolate, stoic, and a killer" (Lawrence 68), are the subject of chapter 3. I focus here on representations of Daniel Boone by John Filson and Timothy Flint, and on James Fenimore Cooper's *Leatherstocking* novels, where we find frontiersmen ranging fluidly and thrivingly between America's pastoral and political *nomos*, the worlds of the "savage Indian" and the "civilized settler." I consider this hybrid figure as a kind of eunomic self-shepherd who, through the effectively sacred ritual of violent confrontation, "presents himself to us as a new man, the author and artificer of his own fortunes" (Flint, *The Life* 12).

Chapter 4 examines Emerson, Thoreau, and Whitman, three unbound celebrants of personal autonomy. Emphasizing their roles as elenchic examiners set apart from the human *nomos*, I note how these authors apotheosize the self-pastured person, yet still retain a faith—essentially Jeffersonian—in the fusion of the pastoral and political. I conclude by juxtaposing these authors' work with writings by Poe and Melville, who, in dramatizing *eunomia*'s dissolution, highlight the potential for pathological violence in an individual's separation from *nomos* and offer premonitions of the self-terminating conditions of hyperautonomy.

In chapter 5, I shift to the twentieth century and works by Ernest Hemingway and Norman Mailer which explore, in the context of eunomic dissolution, vestigial possibilities for productive self-pasture in the autonomous person's separation from *nomos*. Looking first at Hemingway's *In Our Time* (1925), *The Sun Also Rises* (1926), and *A Farewell to Arms* (1929), I survey a self-pasture marked by a cool detachment from the nomistic world and the cultivation of a private (rather than, as for Jefferson, a shared) access to *themis*. Rugged Epicureans, Hemingway's isolates respond to an existential void by treating sensuous experience as the ground of value. Such figures preserve, moreover, the frontiersman's readiness for violence, but in a form that typically resists organization into sacred rituals. In turning to Mailer's valorization of the outlaw in a series of works written during the first three decades of his career—*The Naked and the Dead* (1948), "The White Negro" (1957), *An American Dream* (1965), *The Executioner's Song* (1979)—I demonstrate how he elaborates Hemingway's investigation of the nomistic detachment of the autonomous person, but modifies his precursor, first, by offering an outright celebration of the potential of that figure to challenge, as a heroic existentialist, the rise of coercive nomistic powers; and second, most importantly, by suggesting how dangerous to the conventional nomistic world—how vainly predatory upon it—such a figure is likely to be. While Mailer's outlaws reclaim some of the potency of earlier stages of autonomy, such figures come to seem, his work increasingly concedes, spiritually barren and implicated in unredeemed violence.

With *Blood Meridian*, the focus of chapter 6, we encounter an unambiguously destructive vision of American autonomy. McCarthy's novel uses its nineteenth-century setting in the southwestern borderlands—a moment and place permitting the most extreme expressions of self-law—in order to illustrate American autonomy as it reaches its sublime "meridian" (in several of the word's senses, including that of an apogee, a satanic incarnation, and an utter isolation) and approaches the self-annihilating conditions of its undeath in the late twentieth century. McCarthy's Judge Holden takes Jefferson's "sacred fire" and scorches the earth with it (recalling the Greeks' *nemo* in its sense of fiery consumption), recasting the mythic frontiersman's sacred hunt as a terminal version of Callicles's pitiless "law of nature" and outright rejection of the political *nomos*. The novel also foretells, in the Judge's own pronouncements on the closing of the American frontier, autonomy's last stages and the terminal devolution of American *eunomia*.

Chapter 7, exploring DeLillo's *White Noise* (1985), *Libra* (1988), and *Underworld* (1997), charts autonomy's undeath, a radically centripetal and disintegrative form of "self-pasture" which increasingly involves a pasturing not *by* but *on* the self. McCarthy's dark prophecy in *Blood Meridian*—the effective disappearance of the self within itself, in solitary communion with *themis*—is realized in DeLillo's explorations of hyperautonomy's emergence. Journeying within a weirdly internalized and synthetic Nature, the author's urban desperadoes still claim a privileged, private access to *themis*, but are at once detached from *nomos* (self-lawed in self-pasture, feeding and ranging at will) and absorbed *within* it, since that pasture is now systematically mediated, through unprecedented environmental mastery and disciplinary control, by nomistic powers. The "sacred hunt" now seems to yield, for ordinary citizens, only a banal indulgence of desire, and for the desperately marginal, a senseless eruption of violence. DeLillo represents an advanced stage of eunomic dissolution which repudiates Jefferson's vision of the harmony of individual and communal virtue: "the Laws of Nature," now understood as largely manipulable by humans, no longer nourish the American *nomos*. Here we sense, moreover, autonomy's nascent conceptual disintegration, as the *auto-* in *auto-nomia* begins to weaken and dissolve: with the self's profound implication in technological prosthetics, and the fluidity of self-constructions this makes possible, it becomes difficult to recognize that self *as* a self, at least according to any traditional understanding of the term. Personal auto-nomy seems, in fact, to have returned "person" to its etymological origin as *mere* persona(e). The merging of the self with technology finally amounts to something, in fact, like a self-annihilating auto*matism*.

The epilogue of this study briefly examines Gary Shteyngart's satirical novel *Super Sad True Love Story* (2010) and its representation of hyperautonomy in the context of twenty-first-century information technologies.

The hyperautonomy that DeLillo sketches in its emergent form, when the phenomenon is most clearly visible on the social margins and is just beginning to dominate political life, Shteyngart represents as banally ascendant within the American *nomos*. Posthuman automatons graze here in limitless virtual pastures, even as the nation itself collapses.

1 /   The Birth and Growth of Autonomy
in Ancient Greece

αὐτόνομ-ος *[autonomos]*
A. *living under one's own laws, independent,* of persons and states
2. *generally, of one's own free will*
3. of animals, *feeding and ranging at will*
         —H. G. LIDDELL AND R. SCOTT, *GREEK-ENGLISH LEXICON*

In what follows I offer a brief, heuristic outline—from Homer to Epicurus—of the emergence of personal autonomy in ancient Greek literature, tracing some of the intriguing etymological associations of *auto-nomia* ("self-law," "self-pasture") and the various shades of its root gesture *nemo* ("deal out, dispense, order, or assign," "pasture or tend flocks," "feed upon or graze," "have to oneself or possess," "inhabit," "consume [in a fire]," "spread [like an ulcer]") with the land itself, as well as the evolving idea of law as sanctioned by human or divine powers external to any person. My intent is to set out a sort of archaic anatomy which, I hope, will serve as an illuminating backdrop to the imaginative history of autonomy in America.

Self-lawed states, let alone the phenomena of self-lawed persons, were not part of the early Greek tradition. In the Homeric world, the divine law of Themis (*themis*) rather than any human law (*nomos*) formed the core of the legal structure of mortal communities, while the authority of the greatest human rulers was traced to, and found an external check in, the gods. A famous passage from the *Iliad* (ca. eighth century BCE) makes clear Agamemnon's divine connections by citing the provenance of his scepter, which has been fashioned by Hephaestus himself: "Hephaestus gave it to lord Zeus, son of Cronos, and Zeus gave it to Argeiphontes, the messenger; and Hermes, the lord, gave it to Pelops, driver of horses, and Pelops in turn gave it to Atreus, shepherd of men; and Atreus, dying, bequeathed it to Thyestes, rich in flocks, and Thyestes then left it to

Agamemnon to wield, to be lord of many islands and of all Argos" (*Iliad* 2.102–8). Honorable rule over free citizens typically involved, moreover, a respect for the mutual obligations binding rulers and their subjects. Homer's treatment of rulers often emphasizes the sort of debts they owe their subjects as the price of control over the land. In book 12 of *The Iliad*, the Lycian king Sarpedon explains to his cousin the force of their kingly obligations:

> Glaucus, why is it that the two of us are honored above all with
> prominent seats, and the best food, and flowing wine in Lycia,
> and all men look upon us as on gods? Yes, we possess [*nemomes-*
> *tha*, from *nemo*, as above] a great domain by the banks of Xanthus,
> a rich tract of orchard and of wheat-bearing plough-land. There-
> fore we must take our place among the Lycian front, and face the
> blazing conflict so that many of the mail-clad Lycians might say:
> "Certainly these are not inglorious men who rule in Lycia, even
> our kings, who eat the fat sheep and drink the best, honey-sweet
> wine: no, their might too is great, since they fight among the Lycian
> front." (12.310–21)

Divine dispensation could punish rulers who breached *themis*, and humans had always to be mindful not just of other hostile humans, but of the gods and their ultimately decisive role in mortal affairs. Hence, in book 16 of *The Odyssey*, Amphinomos prudently notes the importance of assessing divine will before committing violence: "Friends, I certainly would not choose to kill Telemachus; it is a terrible thing to kill one of royal stock. No, let us first seek to know the will of the gods. If the divine laws [*themistes*] of great Zeus approve, I will kill him myself, and encourage everyone else in the task; but if the gods are against it, then I ask you to stop" (*Odyssey* 16.400–405). Amphinomos's name—linking *amphi* ("on both sides" or "all around") with *nomos* ("law"/"pasture")—heralds, furthermore, the very actions he performs. As one of the suitors plaguing Penelope, he fulfills his name in two ways: first, by occupying and controlling Odysseus's land, he "grazes all around" (*amphi-nomos*), and second, by respecting both the human convention governing the suitors and the divine prohibition against killing a prince, he invokes "both laws" (*amphi-nomos*).

Two less common, figurative senses of the root gesture *nemo* (both of which bear on the kind of occupation carried out by Amphino-mos and the suitors, and which prefigure late, pathological stages of autonomy's life cycle in American literature) suggest the destructive potential inherent in consumptive possession or control. Just after the catalogue of ships in book 2 of *The Iliad*, Homer uses the word to mean "consume by fire," emphasizing the incendiary effect of the assembled armies: "So they moved ahead as though all the land were engulfed with flames [*nemoito*, literally, "fed upon (by fire)"]; and the earth groaned beneath them, as when Zeus who hurls the thunderbolt in his wrath punishes the land around Typhoeus.... So the earth groaned hugely beneath them as they marched" (*Iliad* 2.780–84). Herodotus uses a form of *nemo* in the sense of a spreading disease: "A short time later, something else happened; there was a swelling on the breast of Atossa, the daughter of Cyrus and wife of Darius, which opened and advanced [*enemeto*, "fed upon"] further" (Herodotus, *Histories* 3.133.1). Human-engendered forces such as military operations might desolate the earth they occupy and negate the sustenance it has provided, just as mysterious diseases might destroy the healthy bodies of which they take possession.

To convey a *place* providing sustenance, Homer uses the noun *nomos* (as "pasturage"). By the end of the eighth century, this word had taken on a new and distinct meaning: *nomos* as divinely established human practice or normative behavior which delineates the moral framework in which one lives. Hesiod's *Works and Days* (ca. 700 BCE) provides the earliest extant appearance of *nomos* in this sense, in a passage distinguishing the *nomos* of human life from that of other animals:

> The son of Cronos [Zeus] has assigned this law [*nomon*] for mankind, that fishes and beasts and winged birds should devour each other, because they do not participate in justice [*dike*]; but to mankind he gave justice, which is greatly superior. Far-seeing Zeus gives prosperity to whomever knows justice and is ready to speak it; but whoever deliberately cheats and perjures himself, and so wounds justice and sins fatally, that man's generation will be thwarted thereafter. (Hesiod, *Works* 274–84)

Unlike animals, humans receive from Zeus a *nomos* which includes the ability to make choices about right and wrong while remaining subject to divine rewards or penalties based on those choices: "For upon the all-nourishing earth Zeus has thirty thousand spirits, those who as they travel over the entire earth, clothed in mist, supervise the judgments and evil deeds of mortal men" (252–55). The context of moral decision making is placed, therefore, beyond individuals as well as communities, and the human *nomos* becomes, we might say, a kind of metaphorical

pasturage in which divine sustenance might be claimed. Hesiod's assertion of Zeus's authority is further reinforced in his retelling of the story
of Prometheus, who defies the sovereign god by giving the gift of fire to
mortals. Outraged by the transgression, Zeus sentences both Prometheus
and mankind to eternal affliction: "Son of Iapetus [Prometheus], greatest
in cunning, you are pleased to have cheated me and stolen fire—but a
great misery this act will be to you and to all mortals. As repayment for
fire I will give men an evil which will delight them, so that they lovingly
embrace their own destruction" (54–58).

By the fifth century BCE, *nomos* takes on an important new meaning
in the context of the nascent Athenian democracy. It supplants the word
thesmos (kin to *themis*) as a signifier of specific laws and customs which
humans are expected to obey, but with an important difference:

> The basic idea of θεσμός [*thesmos*] is . . . that of something imposed
> by an external agency, conceived as standing apart and on a higher
> plane than the ordinary, upon those for whom it constitutes an
> obligation. The sense of obligation is also inherent in νόμος [*nomos*],
> but it is motivated less by the authority of the agent who imposed
> it than by the fact that it is regarded and accepted as valid by those
> who live under it. . . .
>
> This radical difference between the two terms suggests that the
> change from θεσμός to νόμος came about at a time when the Athe-
> nians were disenchanted with living under laws imposed upon
> them from above, and decided instead to consider as laws only
> norms which they had themselves ratified and acknowledged to be
> valid and binding. (Ostwalt 55)

In further contrast to the sense of *nomos* used by Hesiod, *nomos* in the
fifth century BCE and after is associated with human ratification rather
than an appeal to the external sanction of the divine. Laws and customs
come to be understood not as the will of the gods or particular human
rulers claiming to act in accordance with that will, but as manipulable
products of a collective human will. The change marks a profound movement toward secularization, and the auto-nomy of humankind, further
emphasized by the consolidation of laws in written form. By the end of
the fifth century, *nomos*, though still used in other senses, had predomi-
nantly come to mean "statute," a law sanctioned by human practices,
and one which "intended to deprive of legal validity any νόμος [*nomos*]
which was not written and, we may assume, officially published in an
authoritative manner" (1).

We see a portent of the decline of *nomos* if we turn back to Homer, where in book 2 of the *Iliad* the misshapen Thersites, no more than a common soldier, offers a seditious critique of Agamemnon. Accusing his superior of greed and arrogance, Thersites petitions his fellows to abandon the war: "It is not right for a ruler to bring harm to the sons of the Achaeans. Weak fools! Base shameful things, you women of Achaea, men no longer, let us sail homeward with our ships, and leave this fellow here in the land of Troy to enjoy his prizes, so that he may find out whether we help him in any way or not" (*Iliad* 2.234–42). What makes the moment so shocking is its violation of Agamemnon's divinely sanctioned authority in an appeal—proleptically suggestive of the rise of the democratic polis—to the "mass of men" and their collective interests (Karl Marx, for obvious reasons, took a great interest in this scene). The rupture is extraordinary, but does not last long: Odysseus soon violently reasserts themistic rights by beating Thersites over the head with Agamemnon's divinely descended scepter.

Odysseus himself, however, displays a profound ironic detachment *from* this incipient *nomos*. Notorious for his shrewdness and mendacity, his silver tongue and myriad disguises, he is introduced to us in the *Odyssey* as a "man of many devices [*polytropon*]" who "saw the cities, and knew the minds, of many men" (1.1, 3). The favorite of Athena, who sometimes scolds him for his excesses, Odysseus trumpets his own glory as a consummate deceiver, known "for every kind of trick" (9.19). The climax of Odysseus's ten-year adventure in attempting to return home is a scene of mass murder, as he eliminates the suitors who have been plaguing his land and family. Nietzsche, reading Odysseus as a prototype of the overman and rather rashly shrinking the range of Greek ideals, enthusiastically endorses the hero's polytropic endowments: "What did the Greeks admire in Odysseus? Above all, his capacity for lying, and for cunning and terrible retribution; his being equal to contingencies; when need be, appearing nobler than the noblest; the ability to be *whatever he chose*; heroic perseverance; having all means at his command; possession of intellect—his intellect is the admiration of the gods, they smile when they think of it—: all this is the Greek *ideal*! The most remarkable thing about it is that the antithesis of appearance and being is not felt at all and is thus of no significance morally. Have there ever been such consummate actors!" (*Daybreak* 156). In not *feeling* the antithesis of appearance and being, or public and private selfhood, Odysseus is free to transcend it, becoming whatever he needs to in order to survive and flourish. He may be detained and molested by divine antagonists, but he remains happily manipulative of both gods and men when it suits him. An actor who scripts himself, Odysseus ultimately obeys an internal, self-delighting, self-lawed authority, and he moves within the nomistic world as a kind of shifting blankness, adopting and discarding various personae. In tricking the Cyclops Polyphemus, he gives himself a name— "no man"—which fittingly suggests his elusiveness. Odysseus's ease in toying with conventional authority uncannily prefigures, I suggest, the forbiddingly blank "psychopathic types" explored later in this study: like their Homeric predecessor, they tend to be affectively detached from the antithesis of appearance and being, polytropic as they wander into encounters with others, and finally given to "terrible retribution."

In Sophocles's *Antigone* (ca. 442 BCE), which examines a crisis point in conceptions of the legitimate origin and authority of law, we find the first ever appearance of the word *autonomos*. Determined that her brother Polyneices should receive burial, but opposed by the equally determined Creon, who decrees that he shall not, Antigone is herself sentenced to a live burial. As she is led away to execution, the Chorus offers a summation of her fate: "Therefore, carrying glory and praise, you depart for the depths, home of the dead, not wasting away with the terror of some fatal disease, nor having claimed the wages of the sword; no, you were self-lawed [*autonomos*]. Still living, alone among mortals, you will venture to Hades" (Sophocles, *Antigone* 817–22). In explaining her disobedience, Antigone invokes the eternal themistic laws, contrasting them with Creon's merely human *nomos*. By her reckoning, *Creon* is himself claiming an auto-nomous authority in breaching divine law: "It was not Zeus who heralded this, nor Justice [*Dike*], living with the gods below, who laid down such laws among men. I did not think anything you heralded had such force to let a mortal over-rule the unwritten and unfailing laws of the gods [*agrapta kasphale theon nomima*]. For they exist not merely today or yesterday, but eternally, and no one knows when they were first revealed" (450–57). The eunomic fusion of the political and the pastoral is sundered here as the representatives of *nomos* and *themis* clash. Antigone's execution itself provides further commentary on the fate of those who attempt sole possession of the law. Her ostensibly unique descent to the underworld while "still alive"—a rather enigmatic description of death—can be attributed to the specific conditions of the sentence Creon has imposed. In an apparent attempt to absolve himself of some guilt, he has ordered Antigone entombed with food, which she can choose to eat or not, thereby to some extent determining the timing of her own death by starvation. The entombment itself creates a remarkable pun on

Antigone's fierce defense of a higher law: in response to her disobedience, Creon has left her alone, with full control over her sustenance, free to feed and range at will within the space provided her, quite literally self-pastured (*autonomos*).

The extraordinary influence of the Sophists on Greek culture in the latter half of the fifth century BCE contributed to a decline in the authority of *themis*, and to profound changes in how *nomos* was understood. Sophistic pedagogy exposed traditional beliefs to unprecedented scrutiny, undermining the authority of the gods in favor of an understanding of human life and laws in largely human terms. *Nomos* and *physis* ("nature") were commonly invoked antithetically in this period, with the former attributed to rules and conventions established and enforced by human communities, the latter to inviolable principles of the universe (amounting to a kind of radical reduction of *themis* to mere insentient process). Plato's *Gorgias* (ca. 380 BCE) presents the character Callicles as a provocative defender of this denuded *physis* and the new "personal autonomy" that it appears to sanction:

But it seems to me that those who make the laws [*nomous*] are the weaker sort of men, and the more numerous. Thus they aim to serve their own interests when they make their laws [*nomous*] and assign praise and blame, while also threatening the stronger sort of people who otherwise would be able to have an advantage; preventing them from gaining it, they tell them that such greatness is unwholesome and unjust, and that doing wrong involves just this effort to be superior to one's neighbors: they are, of course, quite happy to see themselves on an equal plane, when they are in fact so inferior. This is the reason why, by convention [*nomo*], it is termed unjust and unwholesome to strive for an advantage over the majority, and why they call it wrong: but nature [*physis*], in my opinion, herself proclaims that it is right for the superior to have an advantage over the inferior, and the strong over the weak. This fact is obvious in many situations, not only in the animal world, but among various states and peoples—what is right, it has been determined, is the influence and advantage of the stronger over the weaker. What kind of right did Xerxes obey in marching against Greece, or his father against Scythia? Or consider the countless other similar cases that one might cite. Why, these men certainly follow nature, the nature of right [*physin ten tou dikaiou*], in acting this way; yes, I myself follow the law of nature [*nomon ge ton tes*

physeos], though not that law, of course, which men make themselves. (Plato, *Gorgias* 483b–e)

Note that Hesiod's understanding of the *nomos* applicable to humans
as a divinely sponsored frame for just actions disappears here, with the
predatory conditions of animal life now holding for the human animal
as well. Callicles goes on to claim that the naturally strong are deluded,
by nomistic convention, into forsaking their superiority. He calls for
the rise of the strong from artificial bondage, and with it a thorough
upheaval of social order. What Callicles lauds as "natural justice" (*physeos dikaion*) is literally "nature's (ad-)justment," in the sense that a text
is "justified," that is, made even or balanced: "nature's even-ing," its
"just-ness," its perfect and impartial leveling of all artificial constraints
(a *harma dikaion*, for instance, is a "well-balanced, even-going chariot").
Nomos, Callicles would suggest, is neither a dispensation of the gods nor
an expression of the communal will in the service of justice, but merely
a product of self-interested human manipulation (typically inhibiting
powerful persons like himself). *Physis*, he insists, licenses a transcendent autonomy for which the entire nomistic world is (aggressively con-
tested) pasture. A contemporary analogue of Callicles can be found, I
argue later, in the desolating "naturalism" of Cormac McCarthy's Judge
Holden, who similarly subordinates *nomos* to *physis*—the latter, in its
American formulation, still brutally austere but retaining the force of
themistic obligation—which bloodily pits autonomous wills against one
another, an even-ing redness in the West.

The elenchic Socrates, opponent of the Sophists in the *Gorgias* and
elsewhere, is himself a proponent of autonomous personhood, though
of a profoundly different kind than that of Callicles. Socratic *elenchus*,
a relentless cross-examination which aims to detect and pry open the
logical cracks in one's assumptions, radically exposes *nomos* to personal
skepticism. In the *Apology,* Socrates describes himself as an *idiotes*, a
"private man" who does not work within the public conventions of the
polis—for instance, as a participant in the Assembly or as someone holding a specific political office—but rather devotes himself to work that
is independent of official state affairs. The truth he seeks in philosophy
may finally correspond to and confirm *nomos*, but it is sought—in an
anticipation of, among others, Thoreau—outside the public sphere: "In
order to aim for what is right in a genuine way, a man must, if he is to
keep his life even for a short time, be a private citizen rather than a public man" (32a). Defending himself against the charges laid against him,

Socrates describes his divinely ordained role as ultimately in the service of the polis, likening himself to a gadfly which stings a sluggish horse: "I believe I was fixed to the city by the god in this way, and I proceed to stimulate, and exhort and reproach each of you, continually setting upon you, everywhere, throughout the day" (30e). Though he is accused by Athenian authorities of religious heresy, Socrates claims to have divine sanction for his life as an *idiotes*, having been "ordered to do this by the god through dreams and oracles" (33c). The themistic authority heeded by Socrates is, however, itself *idio*syncratic: he has, he says, had recourse since childhood to an inner voice, a so-called *daemon*, which warns against certain actions.

Socrates's intellectual detachment—and indeed *affective* detachment, which we see most strikingly in his stoical response to his death sentence in the *Crito*—suggests the virtues of a radical kind of self-shepherding (auto-nomy) within the Athenian *nomos*. Plato did not see those virtues, however, as ends in themselves, but in fact as means to reform and revitalize the nomistic world: a project he elaborates in the *Republic*, where complementary classes of citizens, not autonomous agents, form an idealized society. However much (or little) they may succeed in approximating the (themistic) Platonic "forms," the human *nomoi* are, as Plato has Socrates insist in the *Crito*, the parents of the good citizen, the very grounds of self-development, and as such inveterately binding (*Crito* 50c–54d) (the point is advanced yet more forcefully in Plato's later work, the *Laws*). One must not flee one's originary pasture even when, as is finally the case with Socrates, condemned by its rulers. Human flourishing requires, by this reasoning, profound involvement in, and obedience to, human law.

In the teachings of Epicurus (ca. 341–270 BCE), a philosopher born near the time of Plato's death, this key assumption is, however, abandoned. Where Plato—and, of course, his disciple Aristotle—had insisted upon the self's "natural" place within the polis, without which no genuine human flourishing was possible, Epicurus emphasizes the importance of asocial self-protection and self-development. The purpose of life becomes happiness, which he associates with the cultivation of lasting pleasures and the avoidance of those things that might cause pain (including, of course, political involvement). He counsels skepticism toward the gods, and offers material explanations for the physical makeup of the universe. Virtue is lauded not for its own sake, but for its utility in securing one's own happiness. Personal friendships are valued over civic ties. *Ataraxia* (tranquility) and *aponia* (absence of pain) become key goals, and the guiding motto of the Epicureans, according to legend, is *lathe biosas*: "live unobtrusively," that is, enjoy one's life out of the public eye. Isaiah Berlin sums up the significance of this transition from the political philosophy of Plato and Aristotle, which he explores in relation to both Epicurus and Zeno of Citium (ca. 334–262 BCE):

> [In] place of hierarchy, equality; in place of emphasis on the superiority of specialists, the doctrine that any man can discover the truth for himself and live the good life as well as any other man, at least in principle; in place of emphasis on intellectual gifts, ability, skill, there is now stress upon the will, moral qualities, character; in place of loyalty, which holds small groups together, groups molded by tradition and memories, and the organic fitting-in of all their parts and functions, there is a world without national or city frontiers; in place of the outer life, the inner life; in place of political commitment, taken for granted by all the major thinkers of the previous age, sermons recommending total detachment. (Berlin 302–3)

Eunomic dissolution reaches a culminating stage here in the Epicurean privacy forming within the human *nomos*; themistic authority is "privatized" and nomistic authority rejected. *Nomos* is but an expedient for the apolitical self, and *themis* shrunken to the point of irrelevance.

The American experiment with liberty exuberantly revives Socrates's elenchic model and Epicurus's nomistic detachment, associating them with a much larger, more empowered self, given unprecedented access to *themis*. In Jefferson, the mythic frontiersmen, and Emerson, Thoreau, and Whitman, we encounter endorsements of autonomy's positive, fertile possibilities. Brown, Poe, and Melville, in providing a kind of shadow play on autonomy's sunniest dimensions, emphasize its explosiveness and self-annihilating potential, concerns that are elaborated—after the vestigially recuperative efforts of Hemingway and Mailer—by McCarthy, DeLillo, and Shteyngart, who show us a self-pasture spectacularly destructive to self and community alike.

2 /   Eunomia's Rebirth in America

*The pastoral ideal has been used to define the meaning of America ever
since the age of discovery, and it has not yet lost its hold upon the native
imagination. . . . With an unspoiled hemisphere in view it seemed that
mankind actually might realize what had been thought a poetic fantasy.
Soon the dream of a retreat to an oasis of harmony and joy was removed
from its traditional literary context. It was embodied in various utopian
schemes for making America the site of a new beginning for Western
society.*

—LEO MARX, *THE MACHINE IN THE GARDEN*

Thomas Jefferson, mythopoeic draftsman of the American arcadia, was
keenly aware that the nation's "new beginning" was linked to a tradition
of political liberty dating back to the ancients. In a letter to Henry Lee
in 1825, he affirmed both the distinctness and the historical indebtedness
of the Declaration he had penned nearly a half century earlier: "Neither
aiming at originality of principle or sentiment, nor yet copied from any
particular and previous writing, it was intended to be an expression
of the American mind, and to give to that expression the proper tone
and spirit called for by the occasion. All its authority rests then on the
harmonizing sentiments of the day, whether expressed in conversation,
in letters, printed essays, or in the elementary books of public right, as
Aristotle, Cicero, Locke, Sidney, &c." ("To Henry Lee" 1501). An accomplished classical scholar, Jefferson revered the pastoral tradition and
its idealization of rural life. His reading of the classics, along with his
experience of crowded European cities, informed his belief that America would flourish only if it regulated its political affairs according to a
blending of natural and human law. For Jefferson, the divine revealed
itself in and through "the Laws of Nature and of Nature's God" ("Declaration" 19), providing a sustaining moral pasture for those who, if left on
their own to cultivate the natural world under the benevolent sponsor-
ship of the Christian God, would natively incline to goodness. He put the
claim bluntly to James Madison in a letter penned in 1787: "I think our
governments will remain virtuous for many centuries; as long as they are
chiefly agricultural; and this will be as long as there shall be vacant lands

in any part of America. When they get piled upon one another in large cities, as in Europe, they will become corrupt as in Europe" ("To James Madison" [1787] 918). The fusion of the political and the pastoral that Jefferson saw as integral to American virtue—analogous to the Greeks' *eunomia*—was the stage on which the nation's experiment in autonomy would play out.

In his first inaugural address, delivered a quarter century after the Declaration, Jefferson set forth his fundamental conviction that the looser force of government under the American republic—"the world's best hope" ("First Inaugural" 493)—would not create anarchy but instead foster personal and communal virtue. He imagined the nation's citizens bound by nomistic structures that would harmonize the human and the divine (reconstituting, in effect, Hesiod's sense of *nomos* as nourished by *themis*). In contrast to archaic Greece or contemporary Europe, however, themistic authority would not be located in human rulers. An autonomous citizenry would range free of monarchical shepherds, self-lawed in self-pasture.

The *personal* autonomy that develops within the American *nomos* and its eunomic fusion would, in fact, prove much more destructive to both individuals and communities than that known by the ancient Greeks. In Jefferson's rationalism and hostility to religious dogma—partly modeled on Epicurean thought—we discover a prefiguration of the concept's later, more extreme and corrosive stages. The flowering of virtuous agrarian life imagined by Jefferson required, of course, the forcible removal of indigenous populations, the enslavement of Africans, and armed revolution against a tyrannical state power. We may be reminded here of Nietzsche's remark about the origin of "the moral conceptual world": "its beginnings were, like the beginnings of everything great on earth, soaked in blood thoroughly and for a long time" (*Genealogy* 65). Jefferson's optimistic endorsement of reduced human governance might *also* be seen as opening the way for the blood-soaked excesses explored later in this study—dangerous liberties which emerge as *themis* becomes detached from the nomistic world, and personal autonomy, no longer sustained nor profoundly restrained by the human *nomos*, swells to unprecedented proportions.

Jefferson had read deeply in theories of natural law, and he turned to ideas of natural rights in seeking justification for the overthrow of British tyranny.[1] He revered what he took to be universal law—an extension of divine will or *themis*—which guaranteed certain freedoms and generally bequeathed the terms and scope of human law in its local applications. In "A Summary View of the Rights of British America" (1774), Jefferson outlines American complaints about the infringement of its natural rights and highlights the connection between land and liberty. Free movement across land is identified as an important and universal right, asserted historically by the Saxons in moving to Britain and now repeated by the American colonists: "our ancestors, before their emigration to America, were the free inhabitants of the British dominions in Europe, and possessed a right which nature has given to all men, of departing from the country in which chance, not choice, has placed them, of going in quest of new habitations, and of there establishing new societies, under such laws and regulations as to them shall seem most likely to promote public happiness" ("Summary" 105–6). Jefferson goes on to point to "the exercise of free trade with all parts of the world" (108) as another natural right. Legal restrictions on American manufacturing are a despotic violation—he cites in particular a British law prohibiting "an American subject [. . . from making] a hat for himself of the fur which he has taken perhaps on his own soil" (109)—for such laws deny Americans the free use of their land and inhibit economic independence. By settling the "wilds of America . . . at the hazard of their lives, and loss of their fortunes" (107), the colonists had, by natural right, laid claim to self-pasture (auto-nomy).

In the opening paragraph of the Declaration, Jefferson announces the eunomic fusion underlying the American dissolution of prior "political bands," invoking "the laws of Nature and of Nature's God" as sanction for the people's rebellion. The first sentence of the second paragraph—which has achieved a sacred aura in the American imaginary—summarizes the natural rights being asserted: "We hold these truths to be self-evident, that all men are created equal, that they are endowed by their Creator with certain inalienable rights, that among these are Life, Liberty and the pursuit of Happiness" (19). The equality referred to here has, at least since Lincoln's invocation of it in the Gettysburg Address, conventionally been interpreted as a defense of personal rights, and has since been appealed to at crucial stages of American history. While Jefferson of course defended such rights—and, as we shall see, went much further elsewhere in articulating his ideas about their legitimate range—his specific interest here was, as Jack N. Rakove argues, in delineating the power of *corporate* autonomy: "The colonists, as a people, had a natural right to enjoy the same rights of self-government that other peoples did. It was the collective right of revolution and self-government that the Declaration was written to justify—not a visionary or even utopian notion of equality within American society itself" (Rakove 23). The difference in focus Rakove points to is telling, for it suggests the rising importance, since 1776, of *personal* autonomy as the key measure of American liberty.

The Transcendentalists, in whom we find this rise stunningly accelerated, similarly cite "higher laws" in an augmented defense of the *idiotes* ("private man") against what they take to be nomistic despotism. For Emerson, Thoreau, and Whitman, appeals to natural law—much more extravagant than what Jefferson envisioned—would in fact license personal detachment from the American *nomos* altogether, in favor of solitary communion with *themis*, while encouraging the pursuit of happiness on profoundly idiosyncratic—or "idiotic"—terms. The (rather advanced) beginnings of such detachment are, however, apparent in Jefferson's own thought. His "favorite philosopher," Carl J. Richard observes, "was Epicurus" (Richard 187), and he "applauded the Epicurean emphasis upon reason" (188). In setting forth a "Syllabus of the doctrines of Epicurus," Jefferson defines the "Gods" as "an order of beings next superior to man, enjoying in their sphere, their own felicities; but not meddling with the concerns of the scale of beings below them," and affirms that "Utility [is] the test of virtue" and that "Man is a free agent" ("To William Short, with a Syllabus" 1433). Jefferson found in the ancient philosopher a distillation not just of the authentic wisdom of Socrates (which, he insisted, Plato sometimes muddled) but of "everything rational in moral philosophy which Greece and Rome have left us" (1430). Jefferson was, as Peter Augustine Lawler puts it, "a Christian Epicurean, or, more precisely, partly Christian and partly Epicurean" (Lawler 18). To Epicurean rationalism Jefferson merely (the word is not too strong) adds, as a kind of spiritual balance, Jesus's insistence on empathic identification with others: "Epictetus and Epicurus give laws for governing ourselves, Jesus a supplement of the duties and charities we owe to others" (1431). Writing to John Adams in 1820, Jefferson rather touchingly illustrates his dual commitments to rationality and brotherly love: "A single sense may indeed be sometimes deceived, but rarely: and never all our senses together, with their faculty of reasoning. They evidence realities; and there are enough of these for all the purposes of life, without plunging into the fathomless abyss of dreams and phantasms. I am satisfied, and sufficiently occupied with the things which are, without tormenting myself or troubling myself about those which may indeed be, but of which I have no evidence. I am sure that I really know many, many, things, and none more surely than that I love you with all my heart, and pray for the continuance of your life until you shall be tired of it yourself" ("To John Adams" 1444).

Jefferson's letters often show him exposing Christian faith to thoroughgoing skeptical inquiry—a method leading to heresies as profound as his denial of Jesus's divinity—as he sought to establish and abide by the authentic foundations of Christian wisdom. Jefferson was a fiercely independent thinker, and devoted a great deal of energy to revealing truths otherwise obscured by the prism of others' thought. Seeking to claim "the diamond from the dunghill" ("To William Short, with a Syllabus" 1431) of various interpolations of Jesus's teaching, he constructed a small book which omitted all but Jesus's own words in the gospels. He planned to add to it "the Greek, Latin and French texts, in columns side by side," and—in another potential heresy—"subjoin a translation of Gosindi's Syntagma of the doctrines of Epicurus, which [have suffered from . . .] the calumnies of the Stoics and caricatures of Cicero" (1373). Writing to his nephew Peter Carr in 1787, Jefferson expresses his rational approach to questions of religious dogma most candidly: "Fix reason firmly in her seat, and call to her tribunal every fact, every opinion. Question with boldness even the existence of a god; because, if there be one, he must more approve of the homage of reason, than that of blindfolded fear. You will naturally examine first the religion of your own country. Read the bible then, as you would read Livy or Tacitus" ("To Peter Carr" 902). Jefferson endorses here, in the fashion of a gadfly, his own uncompromising skepticism about received opinion, and authorizes the free range of personal inquiry wherever it might lead. His admonition is vividly elaborated by Emerson, who sought his own diamonds in dunghills: "One must be an inventor to read well. . . . The discerning will read, in his Plato or Shakspeare [*sic*], only that least part,—only that authentic utterances of the oracle;—all the rest he rejects, were it never so many times Plato's and Shakspeare's" ("American Scholar" 48–49).

The Socratic and Epicurean dimensions of Jefferson are balanced, of course, by his role as an eminent statesman: he was both a "private man"— an *idiotes* who adored the contemplative life at Monticello, his pastoral retreat—and a politician and legislator, publicly involved in shaping the young nation's ideals as well as its legal structure. The legislative bent of Jefferson, however, anticipated the emphasis on personal rights now attributed to the Declaration in leaning strongly toward protecting personal privacy and independence (as if, one might say, his ideal was to find a mode of government which finally made government unnecessary). Of particular concern was preserving religious liberty against the tyrannical influence of ecclesiastical institutions. Jefferson viewed the influence of contemporary Christian clergy with suspicion, and wished to found religious worship on a rational, "natural" morality. The Virginia Statute for Religious Freedom, drafted by him in 1779 and setting forth his ideas about religious liberty formally and at length, suggests the attraction for him of an extreme libertarianism. The Statute underlines (if inconsistently) the importance of denying governmental involvement in matters of faith, and puts the rational person in sole charge of his own mode of worship. Vincent Phillip Muñoz observes that Jefferson's potent endorsement of religious liberty in the Statute initially (and nonsensically, since the document is itself meant to shape religious opinion) shrinks to nothing the permissible role of government influence: "From the starting point of the freedom of the human mind, Jefferson concludes that 'the opinions of men are not the object of civil government, nor under its jurisdiction.' If taken literally, that doctrine would seem to prohibit the state from undertaking any effort to influence (let alone punish) any type of opinion" (Muñoz 96). Though he clearly does see a role for government in shaping opinion, Jefferson's penchant, in the Virginia Statute and elsewhere, is to preserve persons from external interference so that the most positive senses of auto-nomy might be nurtured: a nourishing "ordering," "feeding upon," and "possession" of one's self-pasture.

In tracing Virginia's religious history in *Notes on the State of Virginia*, Jefferson is careful to emphasize the importance of ecclesiastical persecution in motivating Old World dissenters to settle in America, while also citing particular instances of such persecution in seventeenth-century Virginia, the gradually declining but still oppressive influence of Anglican authority up until the time of the Revolution, and the infelicitous endurance in common law of the means for punishing religious nonconformity. "The error seems not sufficiently eradicated," Jefferson writes, "that the operations of the mind, as well as the acts of the body, are subject to the coercion of the laws. But our rulers can have authority over such natural rights only as we have submitted to them. The rights of conscience we never submitted, we could not submit" (*Notes* 285). For Jefferson, personal religious liberty was a natural right that, if cultivated sincerely and rationally, would pose no danger to, and would in fact benefit, the broader community: "But it does me no injury for my neighbour to say there are twenty gods, or no god. It neither picks my pocket nor breaks my leg" (285). It is, he affirmed, "reason and free enquiry" (285) which help preserve an uncorrupted relationship to moral—and, synonymously, religious—truth. In an 1802 letter affirming that religious practice was indeed an inalienable right, he thus insists that humankind "has no natural right in opposition to his social duties" ("Jefferson's Letter to the Danbury Baptists"), an idea the Transcendentalists, with their profound distrust of the nomistic world, could wholeheartedly endorse. McCarthy, Mailer, DeLillo, and Shteyngart, in tracing this idea's late stages in the American imaginary, anatomize a personal autonomy that can no longer be said to harmonize the cultivation of religious liberty with social duties, and which emerges instead in stark, destructive opposition to a radically disesteemed *nomos*.

Jefferson saw America as a place where natural rights of land ownership and religious worship might be freely claimed, but also as a sort of eunomic middle ground between nature and (over)civilization. Classical models adapted to the rugged New World frontier—from Homer to Theocritus to Aristotle to Virgil—were crucial in defining this vision. Jefferson, as Richard notes, "cherished the pastoral tradition," was well read in ancient treatises on agriculture as well as modern commentaries on them, and "designed his estate [Monticello] to resemble the Roman villas Pliny and Varro had described" (Richard 161). But Jefferson's American pastoralism converted the backward-looking bent of Roman pastoral— written by aristocratic poets memorializing an imagined agrarian life distanced from its actual physical realities—to an optimistic faith in the nation's present and future possibilities as a new arcadia: "[The] same ideology which evoked nostalgia from the imperial literati of Rome could be a source of encouragement to an American sitting on the edge of a fertile and lightly settled continent" (163). For Jefferson, cultivators of the land—hardworking, happy, and classically learned—defined the promise of the young nation. Commenting in a letter to St. John de Crèvecoeur on what he took to be the misattribution of the source of a British manufacturer's technique in wheel making, he trumpets the education of American farmers: "The writer in the paper, supposes the English workman got his idea from Homer. But it is more likely the Jersey farmer got his idea from thence, because ours are the only farmers who can read Homer" ("Crèvecoeur" 878).

Notes offers Jefferson's most extended reflections on the grand potential of America's eunomic fusion of the pastoral and political. The work was partly intended as a defense against the claims of the ill-informed French naturalist Georges-Louis Leclerc, Comte de Buffon, who had claimed that, generally, natural life in the New World was stunted and weak. Jefferson inventories and celebrates Virginia's geography, legal institutions, social conventions, economic structure, and history as he makes the case for the region's unique vitality. In the brief but revealing Query XIX, a section of *Notes* addressing the "present state of manufactures, commerce, interior and exterior trade" (290), he argues against the notion that America ought to develop a significant manufacturing sector. European land has already been developed, and so "Manufacture must therefore be resorted to of necessity not of choice, to support the surplus of their people" (290). In America, Jefferson reasons, the vast quantity of land available for cultivation makes it feasible for the bulk of the nation to be involved in agriculture, a divinely sanctioned pursuit. Next to the introduction and preamble of the Declaration, the following endorsement of agricultural life may be Jefferson's most famous—and most intellectually definitive—words: "Those who labour in the earth are the chosen people of God, if ever he had a chosen people, whose breasts he has made his peculiar deposit for substantial and genuine virtue. It is the focus in which he keeps alive that sacred fire, which otherwise might escape from the face of the earth" (290). Charles A. Miller sees the phrase "sacred fire" as a nod to something even more provocative than Jefferson's libertarian attitude toward religious worship—as, in fact, an endorsement of an "agricultural divinity, pre-Christian and pagan" (Miller 209). At his beloved estate, Jefferson had friezes representing Roman agriculture, while the "glow of the sacred fire itself may be seen in the dome at Monticello, modeled on the temple in Rome dedicated to Vesta, the goddess of the hearth, who brought the sacred fire from Troy and whose priestesses vowed to keep it burning forever" (210). Here, with the kindling of that fire, Eunomia is reborn.

The moral health of a people was, for Jefferson, necessarily dependent on and inseparable from their direct involvement in managing the land; what bred moral corruption was a separation—atheistic in bent—of workers from "their own soil and industry" (290). The greater the proportion of a population that is involved in agriculture, he concludes, the greater will be that population's virtue. Jefferson also reveals an isolationist preference in *Notes*, and his customary optimism about the benefits of agriculture over commercial life, in speculating on the feasibility of avoiding war by renouncing any claim to the sea: "This would make us invulnerable to Europe, by offering none of our property to their prize, and would turn all our citizens to the cultivation of the earth; and, I repeat it again, cultivators of the earth are the most virtuous and independant [sic] citizens" (300–301). Jefferson's antipathy toward the conditions of city life had been sharpened by travels in London and

Paris, where he had been horrified by the squalor of large slums and the oppressive conditions of factory life. America would, he hoped, avoid such perils by incorporating only the absolutely necessary elements of industrial culture, while placing them within a vast and always ascendant natural environment. In his seminal work on American literary responses to industrialism, Leo Marx provides a cogent summary of Jefferson's vision: "From Jefferson's perspective, the machine is a token of that liberation of the human spirit to be realized by the young American Republic; the factory system, on the other hand, is but feudal oppression in a slightly modified form. Once the machine is removed from the dark, crowded, grimy cities of Europe, he assumes that it will blend harmoniously into the open countryside of his native land" (Marx 150). In America, personal and communal health would be guaranteed by pastoral environments in which "Nature's God" nourished human workers. In contrast, the commercial life of urban centers (which Whitman reclaims, and where Mailer's, DeLillo's, and Shteyngart's autonomists will seek a troubled pasture) bred a kind of disaffected nomopathy, providing a vivid illustration of the destructive sense of the Greek verb *nemo* as ulcerous possession: "The mobs of great cities add just so much to the support of pure government, as sores do to the strength of the human body. It is the manners and spirit of a people which preserve a republic in vigour. A degeneracy in these is a canker which soon eats to the heart of its laws and constitution" (291).

Jefferson's presiding aim in *Notes* was, as R. W. B. Lewis suggests, "to make natural history the queen of the sciences, the new metaphysic, and to turn the inquiry of reality into an investigation of natural processes" (Lewis 15–16). Such investigations were not, however, simply cold, scientific enterprises. They revealed a ubiquitous and active divinity in Nature, and profoundly empowered the investigator. Myra Jehlen contrasts Jefferson's enthusiastically (that is, literally, "possessed by a god") *American* response to the natural world in *Notes* with those of the Argentinian Domingo Sarmiento in his *Civilization and Barbarism* (1845) and the Canadian Susanna Moodie in her *Roughing it in the Bush* (1852). Where Sarmiento and Moodie discover an alienating power in the wilderness, deeply hostile to the human, Jefferson's descriptions position him in command of what he confronts in Nature: "His sight seems rather (paradoxically) to illuminate the view, to bring it into visible focus. He chooses the best position from which to see it, scans it, reflects upon it, boasts of it, and interprets it into a story that ends with him, drawing a circle of which he is at once center and encompassing circumference"

(Jehlen 37). Jefferson's mastering sight directly apprehends, and identifies with, "the laws of Nature and of Nature's God"—that is, the American *eunomia*. Such moments anticipate the (even more extreme) "transparent eyeball" passage of Emerson's essay "Nature," Thoreau's account in *Walden* of fusing with the universe while hoeing his bean field, and any number of visionary scenes represented in Whitman's *Leaves of Grass*.

Jehlen's contrast of Jefferson with Moodie—she is said, unlike him, to be "precisely overwhelmed by the power of the scenery, which almost renders her its object or even its captive, pervading her mind, enchanting her, astonishing her, and in its culminating effect, blinding her" (37)—neglects to account, however, for occasional (and profoundly significant) descriptions of sensory excess and loss of control in *Notes*. The strongly amatory quality of Jefferson's descriptions of the natural world—which stand uneasily next to his typical posturing as Enlightenment scholar, providing a scientific assessment of data as reason dictates—emerges in passages which anticipate Romantic affirmations of (extremely volatile) feeling and idiosyncratic insight. Jefferson's account of the geological formation known as the Natural Bridge, for instance, invokes the sublime. Peering over the edge of the bridge "into the abyss," he tells of being, for a time, perceptually overwhelmed: "Looking down from this height about a minute, gave me a violent head ach [*sic*]. If the view from the top be painful and intolerable, that from below is delightful in an equal extreme. It is impossible for the emotions arising from the sublime, to be felt beyond what they are here: so beautiful an arch, so elevated, so light, and springing as it were up to heaven, the rapture of the spectator is really indescribable!" (148).

We also see the dark, Romantic potential of Jefferson's conception of liberty—briefly but with searing vividness—in two infamous passages from his private correspondence, both of which link the violent struggle for independence with natural imagery. The first, written from Paris in 1787 and known as the "Tree of Liberty" letter, reflects on what came to be known as Shays' Rebellion, an armed uprising by debt-ridden Massachusetts farmers:

> [Can] history produce an instance of rebellion so honourably conducted? I say nothing of it's [*sic*] motives. They were founded in ignorance, not wickedness. God forbid we should ever be 20 years without such a rebellion. The people cannot be all, & always well informed. The part which is wrong will be discontented in proportion to the importance of the facts they misconceive. If they remain

EUNOMIA'S REBIRTH IN AMERICA / 37

quiet under such misconceptions it is a lethargy, the forerunner of
death to the public liberty. We have had 13. states independent 11.
years. There has been one rebellion. That comes to one rebellion in
a century & a half for each state. What country before ever existed
a century & a half without a rebellion? & what country can preserve
it's [sic] liberties if their rulers are not warned from time to time
that their people preserve the spirit of resistance? Let them take
arms. The remedy is to set them right as to facts, pardon & pacify
them. What signify a few lives lost in a century or two? The tree of
liberty must be refreshed from time to time with the blood of patriots & tyrants. It is it's [sic] natural manure. ("To William S. Smith"
911)

Living abroad, Jefferson could idealize America's rebellious spirit and
speak with some glibness of revolutionary violence back home. In the
so-called "Adam and Eve" letter, he goes much further in positing, in a
startling thought experiment, what sacrifices might be justified in the
pursuit of liberty. As minister to France from 1785 to 1789, Jefferson knew
the corruption of the French government firsthand, and was familiar
with the early stages of that nation's revolution. The eventual bloodiness
of the cause doused the sympathy of many of his peers, but Jefferson's
enthusiasm was remarkably intransigent. In 1793, at a point when the
mass slaughter of innocents was well known to him, he penned, from
Philadelphia, the following:

In the struggle which was necessary, many guilty persons fell
without the forms of trial, and with them some innocent. These
I deplore as much as any body, & shall deplore some of them to
the day of my death. But I deplore them as I should have done had
they fallen in battle. It was necessary to use the arm of the people, a machine not quite so blind as balls and bombs, but blind to
a certain degree. A few of their cordial friends met at their hands
the fate of enemies. But time and truth will rescue & embalm their
memories, while their posterity will be enjoying that very liberty for which they would never have hesitated to offer up their
lives. The liberty of the whole earth was depending on the issue of
the contest, and was ever such a prize won with so little innocent
blood? My own affections have been deeply wounded by some of
the martyrs to this cause, but rather than it should have failed, I
would have seen half the earth desolated. Were there but an Adam

& an Eve left in every country, & left free, it would be better than as
it now is. ("To William Short" 1004–5)

A primal pasture for two would be acceptable, affirms Jefferson, in a
reductio ad absurdum whose absurdity seems concealed from him by
the flames of his passion, even if fertilized by the blood of all other
humans.

In a polemical but persuasive analysis of Jefferson's rhetoric in the
"Adam and Eve" letter, Conor Cruise O'Brien paints Jefferson as a
frightening religious zealot, solely committed to the god Liberty and
ready to tolerate any amount of violence in her name. O'Brien accord-
ingly assigns Jefferson a very unflattering contemporary analogue: "It
is difficult to resist the conclusion that the twentieth-century statesman whom the Thomas Jefferson of January 1793 would have admired
most is Pol Pot" (O'Brien 149). Jefferson's contemporary Edmund Burke
articulated similar concerns about the French Revolution itself, whose
spirit he classified under the rubric of the "false sublime." While the
"authentic sublime" involves experience that generates a bracing pleasure and humbling sense of human limits, for Burke the "false sublime"
of the revolutionary period embraces limitlessness and human infinitude. All ultimate externalities vanish in this scheme, which in elevat-
ing the self to imperial status, effectively commands the "sacred fire"
of an oxymoronic private *themis*, and finds a mandate to displace—or
consume, in the sense of *nemo* as consumptive fire—whatever stands
in its way.

The transition to a human-centered sublime finds enthusiastic proponents in Emerson, Thoreau, and Whitman, who see personal autonomy
as a means of revivifying both the self *and* the nomistic world. These
authors find rapture alone in Nature, though their atomistic and centrifugal declarations (which assume an "individuality," separate and
blank, inscribed by Nature) advise a more radical, personalized cultivation of the present in pursuit of fertile self-pasture than that glimpsed in
Jefferson. In the figure of Judge Holden, Cormac McCarthy furnishes a
scathing critique of personal autonomy and its implications for human
communities as well as the natural environment. Here Jefferson's faith
in negative liberty (the self's freedom from government interference)
as a means to positive liberty (the realization of the self's potential, in
solitude as well as communion with other selves) is dramatically annihi-
lated. An ultimate lawgiver who seems bent on making Jefferson's gory
reverie real (minus Eve), the Judge will convert the "false sublime" to an

even more extreme American version: not a "regime's will"—of which Burke had warned—but a single self's, unencumbered by limits, pasturing freely and destructively on the nomistic world, in the sacred fire's blood meridian.

Charles Brockden Brown sent a copy of his Gothic novel *Wieland* to Jefferson in 1798, along with a letter expressing the hope that the vice president would be able to overcome any prejudice he might harbor against reading fiction. "I am conscious," writes Brown, "that this form of composition may be regarded by you with indifference or contempt, that social and intellectual theories, that the history of facts in the processes of nature and the operations of government may appear to you the only laudable pursuits" (Brown, "Letter" 313). Brown politely adds that "his own opinions are different" when it comes to the intellectual seriousness of "fiction," but he does not press the point; instead, he lauds the "artful display of incidents, the powerful delineation of characters and the train of eloquent and judicious reasoning" of his own novel, and speculates that if Jefferson were to begin reading it, he would discover reasons to go on, and, ultimately, judge the time well spent.

Brown's novel *does*, in fact, seem quite serious about exploring "social and intellectual theories" and "the processes of nature and the operations of government," and its subtitle, *The Transformation: An American Tale*, seems to argue for the narrative's national relevance. Though there is no evidence that Jefferson even attempted to read *Wieland*, we can understand why he might have found the work, regardless of its aesthetic value, contemptible. The novel not only focuses on a grisly crime, but it locates the genesis of that crime in the spiritual orientation of a family, living on an idyllic rural estate, with pronounced commitments to classical education and religious liberty. The elder Wieland, we learn, advocated religious pluralism: "His own system was embraced not, accurately speaking, because it was the best, but because it had been expressly prescribed to him. Other modes, if practiced by other persons, might be equally acceptable" (13). Moreover, a separation from others was imperative, he believed, in religious affairs: "He rigidly interpreted that precept which enjoins us, when we worship, to retire into solitude, and shut out every species of society. According to him devotion was not only a silent office, but must be performed alone" (12). These liberties have not, apparently, won divine favor for the Wieland patriarch: outdoors, alone at prayer, he seems, we are informed, to have spontaneously combusted.

The Wieland children, Theodore and Clara, were given great latitude in their own spiritual development: "Our education," Clara confesses, "had been modeled by no religious standard. We were left to the guidance of our own understanding, and the casual impressions which society might make upon us. . . . It must not be supposed that we were without religion, but with us it was the product of lively feelings, excited by reflection on our own happiness, and by the grandeur of external nature" (20). For the Wielands, the "Laws of Nature and of Nature's God" ultimately produce an ironic bounty in Theodore—from Greek *theos* ("god") and *doron* ("gift")—whose "skill in Greek and Roman learning was exceeded by that of few" (40), and whose special interest in "the Daemon of Socrates" culminates in his obedience to an inner voice urging him to massacre his family. Pressed for an explanation, Theodore claims to have achieved an unrestricted, private access to themistic authority: "For a time, my contemplations soared above earth and its inhabitants. I stretched forth my hands; I lifted my eyes, and exclaimed, O! that I might be admitted to thy presence; that mine were the supreme delight of knowing thy will, and of performing it! The blissful privilege of direct communication with thee, and of listening to the audible enunciation of thy pleasure!" (125). The experience, besides leading to senseless destruction, is also finally incommunicable: "The lineaments of that being, whose veil was now lifted, and whose visage beamed upon my sight, no hues of pencil or of language can pourtray [*sic*]" (236).

Theodore's outrages are apparently set in motion—though the precise causal relation is unclear—by the manipulations of a character named Carwin, who has cultivated the ability to disguise and project others' voices. Carwin first appears dressed as a rustic, and Clara's response to him echoes Jefferson's idealization of the "yeoman" farmer in *Notes*: "I reflected on the alliance which commonly subsists between ignorance and the practice of agriculture, and indulged myself in airy speculations as to the influence of progressive knowledge in dissolving this alliance, and embodying the dreams of poets. I asked why the plough and the hoe might not become the trade of every human being, and how this trade might be made conducive to, or, at least, consistent with the acquisition of wisdom and eloquence" (42). Carwin plots to rape Clara, and has himself been convicted of murder and robbery overseas, but the Wielands show themselves to be fatally incapable of comprehending the threat he poses. The novel, as Shirley Samuels has suggested, can plausibly be read as arguing for the importance of institutions which preserve nomistic bonds: Carwin, an "alien" menace to the American arcadia, also "stands (in) for an internal one, the infidelity of religious and institutional beliefs that the novel first appeared to celebrate. If the family had been properly inoculated against him, he could have had no effect on them" (Samuels 395).

With *Wieland*, Brown offered Jefferson a harrowing illustration of the threat posed by personal autonomy in the young republic, countering the Epicurean rationalist's trust in reason and the senses as the foundation for reduced human governance. In positing the sinister potential in nomistic detachment, the work anticipates Poe and Melville's "shadowplay" on Transcendental optimism in the nineteenth century, as well as a devil's brew of literary outlaws in the twentieth and twenty-first centuries.

3 /   The Mythic Frontiersman

*The brash explicitness of American capitalism remains true in spirit
to the revolutionary cataclysm which brought it to birth—one which is
anyway too recent to live down. Insurrection lives on in the form of restless
innovation and robust enterprise. The pioneer spirit was displaced rather
than dissolved. The epic rapacity which subdued the land in the first place
carried on as regular business. Probably no other people on earth use
the word "aggressive" in such a positive fashion, and no group outside
psychoanalytic circles is so fond of the word "dream."*

—TERRY EAGLETON, *HOLY TERROR*

In his *Letters from an American Farmer* (1783), J. Hector St. John de
Crèvecoeur celebrated American autonomy, and in particular the virtuous character of agrarian life, in terms largely parallel to Jefferson's.
Crèvecoeur also warned, however, of the dangers of venturing too far
from civilization, and of giving up the ennobling discipline of agriculture in favor of hunting. So-called "back settlers," aimless and dangerous
frontiersmen, absorbed the "surrounding hostility" of the uncultivated
wilderness and became "ferocious, gloomy, and unsocial," every aspect
of their lives notable for its "lawless profligacy" (51). These unman-
nered and unproductive folk exist in something like the world Callicles
dreamed of—with the lawless "laws of nature," unrestrained by nomistic
conventions, favoring the strong as they seek to dominate the weak—but
they represent for Crèvecoeur a betrayal and negation of autonomy, the
worst of New World possibilities.

A much different representation of the type can be found in Lord
Byron's construction of Daniel Boone in the eighth canto of *Don Juan*.
Writing in the early 1820s—at a distance from America even greater than
Crèvecoeur's, and informed by highly idealized Romantic affirmations
of Natural Man—Byron transforms the frontiersman into a pastoral
archetype, "happiest amongst mortals anywhere" (8.61), "An active her-
mit, even in age the child / Of Nature . . . " (8.63). Boone is lauded for
founding a utopian community—armed but never unnecessarily violent—beyond the corrupting influence of urban life:

LXV.

He was not all alone: around him grew
A sylvan tribe of children of the chase,
Whose young, unawaken'd world was ever new,
Nor sword nor sorrow yet had left a trace
On her unwrinkled brow, nor could you view
A frown on Nature's or on human face; —
The free-born forest found and kept them free,
And fresh as is a torrent or a tree.

LXVI.

And tall, and strong, and swift of foot were they,
Beyond the dwarfing city's pale abortions . . . (8.65–66)

Had Jefferson been a poet, this last line could have been his. Autonomy finds its idyllic representatives here in the American wilds, the laws of nature perfectly harmonized with a sylvan *nomos*.

Two mythic frontiersmen—the legendary Boone, as constructed by John Filson in the late eighteenth century and Timothy Flint in the early nineteenth, and Natty Bumppo, the central protagonist of James Fenimore Cooper's *Leatherstocking* novels (1823–41)—augment Byron's celebration of the frontiersman against Crèvecoeur's monitory portrait of the "back settler," while also revealing important developments in the growth of eunomic autonomy. Self-shepherds in the American arcadia, these frontiersmen range between the "civilized" and "savage" worlds—the former bound by *nomos*, the latter offering free communion with the themistic potency of the wilderness—as they pursue the sacred ritual of the hunt. Boone and Bumppo are ultimately tragic figures, anachronistic and doomed to extinction in developing urban worlds, but their narratives affirm the allure of a detachment from (urban) nomistic conventions, and the cultivation, guided by natural law, of a rugged self-pasture. Significantly, personal autonomy clearly gains ascendance over its corporate counterpart in such figures, for they bring to Jefferson's endorsement of agrarian laborers as "the chosen people of God," and hostility to the corrupting values of commercial centers, a new emphasis on *solitary predation* as a means of communing with the divine.

In the decades after the Revolution, the ideals of the mythic frontiersman were in fact adapted to the very urban environments the figure was imagined as rejecting. Odyssean pragmatism and ruthlessness became identified with entrepreneurial success, heralding a dangerous eunomic dissolution.

Daniel Boone was, of course, an actual explorer, soldier, and pioneer who helped settle the Commonwealth of Kentucky in the 1770s and 1780s. His efforts ultimately opened up vast areas of the continent to national expansion and the agricultural and urban life he despised. In arguing for the profound significance of Boone in the "making of America," Meredith Mason Brown cites his contributions to "the birth of the nation, the westward growth of American territory and of the American settlers, the shrinking of Indian power, the shift from hunting to farming and commerce, the increasing sense of national identity" (Brown 283). It was, as Brown demonstrates, the *idea* of Boone (rather than his own ideas or actions) which helped propel these transformations. By the end of the eighteenth century, Boone had become as much myth as man, celebrated in sometimes fantastical folk tales and literary accounts of his life and exploits. The first of the latter was John Filson's "The Adventures of Col. Daniel Boon [*sic*]," an appendix to his *The Discovery, Settlement and Present State of Kentucke* (1784). Filson delivers, in a formal voice quite his own, Boone's ostensible autobiography, detailing his importance in the historical process that brought white civilization to the region. Kentucky presented itself to early settlers, the narrative insists, as a place of pastoral retreat, extraordinarily fertile and abundantly populated with game: "Nature was here a series of wonders, and a fund of delight" (Filson 52). Filson's Boone embodies the ideal of the American "natural man," at home in this environment, committed to hunting as the fulfillment of human potential, and suspicious of urban life. Surrounded by nature's fecundity, Filson's Boone discovers that potential as no urban dweller could:

> One day I undertook a tour through the country, and the diversity
> and beauties of nature I met with in this charming season, expelled
> every gloomy and vexatious thought. . . . I kindled a fire near a
> fountain of sweet water, and feasted on the loin of a buck, which
> a few hours before I had killed. . . . Thus I was surrounded with
> plenty in the midst of want. I was happy in the midst of dangers
> and inconveniences. In such a diversity it was impossible I should
> be disposed to melancholy. No populous city, with all the varieties
> of commerce and stately structures, could afford so much pleasure
> to my mind, as the beauties of nature I found here. (56)

Like Jefferson rambling in the Virginian outdoors (though now with an explicitly predatory dimension), Filson's Boone encounters a themistic presence in this natural beauty, which grants him spiritual possession of the world before him. Detached from any human community, the frontiersman achieves a personal autonomy suggestive of two unequivocally positive senses of the Greek verb *nemo*: in his relationship to the Kentuckian pasture, he takes the land into his own possession, feeding upon and richly nourished by it. As Richard Slotkin explains of Boone's conversion experience and its relevance to his audience: "Filson's God makes himself apparent through the landscape, and the Word of God becomes apparent to the reader as the landscape alters Boone's attitude gradually from gloom to light and peace. Boone ascends from the wilderness to a commanding height, from which he can view the wilderness at a distance and (figuratively) take in the whole vista of Kentucky" (Slotkin, *Regeneration* 282). The visionary moment prefigures the pastoral experiences of the Transcendentalists, who also find God in solitary natural encounters (a key difference being, of course, that in doing so they posit much larger selves—less humbled in the face of the divine—than Filson's Boone).

For Filson, Native Americans epitomize, in one respect, "natural" living; Boone has learned from (and finally outdone) them in their understanding of how to flourish within the natural world. However, these prior residents of the land—"the numerous warriors that were every where [*sic*] dispersed through the country, intent upon doing all the mischief that savage barbarity could invent" (Filson 62)—also pose the greatest danger to the frontiersman, and it is in armed combat against them that he must fight for his survival. Warfare and exposure to the brutal conditions of the wilderness are, Filson's Boone affirms, essential in realizing the American arcadia: not only is the *land* claimed through such battles, but also an empowered Janusian character for the frontiersman, one which blends the orderliness of white civilization with the supposed primitive vigor of Native American life. It is here that we discover a distinctively American adaptation of pastoral conventions: Nature and its representatives, as Leo Marx points out in citing the work of Cooper, Melville, Faulkner, and Thoreau, emerge in a genuinely "wild" and dangerous form, which the pastoral protagonist encounters not as a shepherd but as a *hunter* (Marx 246n). Extended solitude and violent encounters become part of the American pastoral experience, and an emphasis on *personal* autonomy begins to dwarf its corporate counterpart.

Timothy Flint, musing on Boone's mythic potential in 1826, lamented the absence of a contemporary epic bard equal to the subject: "[Although] much has been said in prose, and sung in verse, about Daniel Boon [*sic*], this Achilles of the West wants a Homer, worthily to celebrate his exploits" (Flint, *Recollections* 67). Flint took on the Homeric role himself in his *Biographical Memoir of Daniel Boone, the First Settler of Kentucky* (1833), lauding the frontiersman as one who had "received his commission for his achievements and his peculiar walk from the sign manual of nature" (Flint, preface to *The Life*). Leaving his human community, Flint's Boone discovers in the Kentucky wilds a "new hunter's paradise" (24), wholly re-creating himself, and inaugurating new human possibilities, within it: "[Boone] presents himself to us as a new man, the author and artificer of his own fortunes, and showing from the beginning rudiments of character, of which history has recorded no trace in his ancestors" (12). Out of Nature comes the new American man.

More rugged and less abstractly philosophical than the man Filson had represented, Flint gives us a Boone who may battle Native Americans, but maintains deep sympathies for their way of life, emulating it himself as he distances himself from white civilization. The wilderness is for him "as the garden of God" (52), and he worships there the Great Spirit, "for the woods were his books and his temple; and the creed of the red men naturally became his" (240). (Flint assures us, however, that "there can be but little doubt, had the gospel of the Son of God been proposed to him, in its sublime truth and reasonableness, that he would have added to all his other virtues, the high name of Christian" [240]). Flint notes that those who enter remote sections of Tennessee and Kentucky, "in their state of extreme isolation from the world they had left" (106), are morally improved, and they become able, *because* of such isolation, to judge and reform the nomistic world left behind. The process is familiar as the movement of retreat from the social into the welcoming fecundity of Nature, followed by an invigorated return, common to the pastoral genre—but, again, with the American emphasis on Nature's wildness and the pastoral protagonist's necessarily violent potential. Flint's Boone, like Filson's, epitomizes the American pastoral hero as solitary hunter. Wandering alone in search of prey, he communes with the divine and realizes his personal potential in surviving hazardous encounters. He is able to thrive in the wilderness because of skills learned from Native Americans, whom he is also, because of his superior white cunning, able to outwit. Not, finally, *of* the white or Native American worlds, the frontiersman moves between them as it suits him.

Flint likens his hero to Achilles, but an even more apt parallel is Odysseus, for Boone, extraordinarily wily as well as rugged, demonstrates a polytropism that would have impressed the ancient "man of many devices" who "saw the cities, and knew the minds, of many men" (*Odyssey* 1.1, 3). Like Odysseus, Flint's Boone seems fully to come into himself, exercising his talents most vividly when using his understanding of nomistic codes, genius for interpersonal manipulation, and facility with disguise to wriggle free of captivity or simply indulge his self-delighting mischievousness. As Flint writes of Boone's escape from the Shawnees: "He would never have acquitted himself successfully, but for a wonderful versatility, which enabled him to enter into the spirit of whatever parts he was called upon to sustain; and a real love for the hunting and pursuits of the Indians, which rendered what was at first assumed, with a little practice, and the influence of habit, easy and natural" (137). Such talents parallel what the Greeks, according to Nietzsche, found praiseworthy in Odysseus: "the ability to be *whatever he chose*" (*Daybreak* 156). And like his ancient antecedent, Flint's Boone is, in a profound sense, an actor, smoothly assuming those roles which assist him in surviving and flourishing. He is, at last, not just a *new* man but a dangerous "no man."

The rich pasture Flint's Boone inhabits and reveres—his eunomic paradise in the woods—is, however, continually encroached upon by settlements and what he takes to be their morally corrosive laws. The contrast he draws between "social life and that of the woodsman" (41) is memorably stark: on the one hand, "the beautiful influences of the indulgence of none but natural desires and pure affections," and on the other, "the selfishness, vanity, and fear of ridicule, that are the harvest of what is called *civilized and cultivated* life" (41). As settlements approach him and make their presence felt, Flint's Boone withdraws ever more deeply into the remaining wilderness. The great paradox of his existence is his involvement in claiming the land from Native Americans and thus opening "an asylum for the oppressed, the enterprising, and the free of every land" (226)—that is, the very people whose life and social institutions he detests. Flint emphasizes the fragility of the eunomic ideal in his narration of the end of Boone's life: crafty lawyers thrust him off his land and out of edenic Kentucky. Boone then ventures to Missouri, where at last we find him resigned to the inevitability of civilized encroachments.

Boone's descendants in the twentieth century inherit this late-stage complication in the expression of rugged autonomy. In Hemingway's isolates, the solitude of the autonomous person becomes much more precarious—a desperate, endangered sanctuary from the threats of the nomistic world—and violence no longer seems reliably connected to its sacred, regenerative potential. Mailer celebrates a version of the "hunter" he calls the "white negro," who brings his polytropic skills to the city in search of opportunities—if increasingly complex ones—for communion with *themis* and the expression of predatory aggression, while putting them in the service of something akin to the Transcendentalists' gigantic, effectively deified self. This figure, the product of another sort of racial blending, is energized by what Mailer takes to be African American "primitivism" (particularly focused, he argues, in sexual potency). DeLillo, nullifying Mailer's optimism about urban frontiersmen, presents us with contemporary Odysseans who roam blankly through cities, without a home to yearn for, senselessly explosive and void of higher purpose.

James Fenimore Cooper's *Leatherstocking* novels introduce Nathaniel "Natty" Bumppo, an American frontiersman who adds significant nuance and depth to the Boone myth. Like Boone, Bumppo (in his various aliases as Deerslayer, Hawkeye, Leatherstocking, Pathfinder, La Longue Carabine, the trapper) cultivates personal autonomy as he ranges between, but is never beholden to, white and Native American worlds. His interracial friendship with the Native American Chingachgook— perhaps Cooper's most significant addition to the myth—nevertheless reinforces many of the frontiersman's familiar qualities: his affinity for the "disorganized" and mobile life of Native Americans, and his avoidance, through a same-sex partnership which supersedes all others, of the entangling responsibilities of family and conventional white civilization. Bumppo's special endowment as "a man without a cross" (*Last* 73) is to exemplify the wisdom and frontier skills of Native Americans (who, again like Boone, he surpasses) as he communes with the divinity and rejuvenating power of the natural world. Bumppo, in short, reaps the spiritual bounty of the American arcadia while remaining white.

Cooper alludes to Boone in an early section of *The Prairie* (1827), a novel exploring the movement of American settlers into the new Louisiana Territory:

Thousands of elders, of what were then called the New States, broke up from the enjoyment of their hard earned indulgencies, and were to be seen leading long files of descendants, born and reared in the forests of Ohio and Kentucky, deeper into the land, in quest of that which might be termed, without the aid of poetry, their natural and more congenial atmosphere. The distinguished and resolute forester who first penetrated the wilds of the latter state, was of the number. This adventurous and venerable patriarch was now seen making his last remove; placing the "endless river" between him and the multitude, his own success had drawn around him, and seeking for the renewal of enjoyments which were rendered worthless in his eyes, when trammeled by the forms of human institutions. (*Prairie* 11)

Cooper's Bumppo, too, flees the oppressive nomistic world; though an octogenarian in this novel, he leaves New York State because he can hear the sounds of human construction near his home. Jefferson's orchestration of the Louisiana Purchase, meant to head off international rivalries in the region and also provide expanded possibilities for "the chosen people of God" to "labour in the earth" (*Notes* 290), offers Cooper's Boone and Bumppo the chance to enjoy the life of the hunter before others arrive to spoil the solitude. The novel shows Bumppo surviving frontier conditions—outwitting inimical Native Americans in Odyssean fashion, often by using strategies he has learned from them—and reaffirming a natural vitality before, at last, dying nobly within a welcoming Pawnee village.

The Last of the Mohicans (1826) recounts Bumppo's adventures as a much younger man during the French and Indian Wars of 1757, and goes further than *The Prairie* in insisting and elaborating on the mortal challenges posed by the frontier environment, as well as its toughening effect on those who live and fight there. Colonists and European soldiers learn survival skills from Native Americans, whose "patience and self-denial" (*Last* 11) form the moral code of the wilderness. A rugged set of values—most notably, a stoic resolve in the face of physical hardship, and an ease with quick and unself-conscious transitions to violence—emerges from the land itself. Bumppo's immersion in the natural world reveals to him the sacredness of active participation in the hunt, and a frontier ethic which limits aggression and values any life one takes. One flourishes here by obeying the strict—but finally invigorating—"laws of nature," which are not starkly Calliclean, brutally setting all against all, but instead retain a guiding, limiting themistic potency. European and colonial penetration into the land is, in the eroticized terms of imperial conquest, the stimulus for a hardened, (blood)lusty masculinity (even if sometimes compromised by the scheming manipulations of foreign overseers): "it would seem that, in time, there was no recess of the woods so dark, nor any secret place so lovely, that it might claim exemption from the inroads of those who had pledged their blood to satiate their vengeance, or to uphold the cold and selfish policy of the distant monarchs of Europe" (11).

Bumppo's ultimate tragedy is that the successful domination of the land makes the frontiersman and his code obsolete. Settled communities subjugate personal, eunomic autonomy, and the "laws of nature" on which the frontiersman's code is based, to the mundane calculus of the human *nomos*. In *The Pioneers* (1823), the aged Bumppo confronts Judge Marmaduke Temple, a wealthy landowner who seeks to impose restrictions on hunting. Bumppo considers himself free of the conventions of white society which regulate space and hunting rights, for he has lived most of his adult life in the wilderness apart from human governance. The proper bounds of his own hunting—the terms of his autonomy or self-pasture—are suggested not by an abstract law which sees the natural world as a commodity to be regulated, but by a respect for the sacred pursuit of prey according to individual need. Bumppo thus scolds another man for unnecessarily slaughtering pigeons: "It's much better to kill only such as you want, without wasting your powder and lead, than to be firing into God's creatures in this wicked manner.... I don't relish to see these wasty ways that you are all practysing, as if the least thing wasn't made for use, and not to destroy" (*Pioneers* 237). In responding to Temple, Bumppo invokes a divinely sanctioned natural law superior to what he takes to be Temple's merely local and human law: "Game is game, he who finds may kill; that has been the law in these mountains for forty years, to my sartain knowledge; and I think one old law is worth two new ones" (153). Temple, of course, sees himself not just as the enforcer of human laws, but as a representative of a different themistic authority, the Christian God who sanctions white civilization in its conflict with the "savage" life Bumppo partly represents. For him, Bumppo is a revolutionary against civic order—the Jacobins have just been invoked in an earlier conversation—while Bumppo sees *him* as violating the transcendent (and divine) law of nature. A deep tension becomes visible here in the eunomic fusion of the political and pastoral. The standoff marks the end of the frontiersman's liberty to range at will: Bumppo is eventually placed in the stocks as punishment and finally vanishes, becoming a martyr to personal autonomy at a historical moment when the frontiersman's liberty has become aggravatingly incompatible with the settlers' life.

Though Bumppo is an elderly man in *The Pioneers* (the first of the *Leatherstocking* novels), and dies in the third, *The Prairie*, the last two novels in the series, *The Pathfinder* (1841) and *The Deerslayer* (1842), return him to earlier stages of his life, thus enacting a mythic process of renovation—or what D. H. Lawrence resonantly dubbed "a gradual sloughing of the old skin, towards a new youth [which is . . .] the myth of America" (Lawrence 60). In *Deerslayer*, the "natural" lessons Bumppo might teach white civilization figure prominently. Bumppo is fully initiated into the wilderness, and at last claims his manhood, by killing an Indian in a deadly standoff. After shooting the man, he cradles him in his arms and receives from him a new name, "Hawkeye." He wakens, as a result of his killing, into a new life: "By this time the sun had not only risen, but it had appeared over the eastern mountains, and was shedding a flood of glorious light on this, as yet, unchristened sheet of water. The whole scene was radiant with beauty, and no one unaccustomed to the ordinary history of the woods, would fancy it had so lately witnessed incidents so ruthless and barbarous" (*Deerslayer* 129). Late in the novel, Bumppo is pointedly asked by a young girl why he violated, in another conflict with a Native American, the biblical commandment against murder. His defense cites his commitment to the sanctioned violence of the wilderness code: "But you must remember, gal, that many things are lawful in war, which would be onlawful in peace. . . . 'Twould have been ag'in natur' not to raise a hand in such a trial, and 'twould have done discredit to my training and gifts" (486). Those gifts also prohibit, of course, acts of mere vengeance: unlike two other unprincipled white characters in *Deerslayer*, Henry March and Thomas Hutter, Bumppo submits to restraints on his aggression, and will kill other men only in self-defense, as part of the severe exigencies of warfare.

Bumppo's essential discovery, the philosophical core of his "training and gifts," is the moral primacy of the natural world, which trumps all forms of merely human wisdom (or put another way, he comes to understand how "Nature's God" takes precedence over man's). As Slotkin summarizes the frontiersman's sacred revelation: "Through his trusting immersion he discovers truths about himself and his world that were hitherto hidden to him; his discriminations are now more just, less the result of habit. In solitude and isolation his acts of war and hunting awake him to his kinship with creation, to a sense of reality and of religious and social duty. His heart is cleansed of evil impulses, and his reason is clarified, strengthened, more dominant over his passions" (Slotkin, *Regeneration* 506–7). The result is the creation of what Flint had prophesied, America's "new man," a version of R. W. B. Lewis's American Adam, his rebirth "accomplished appropriately in the forest on the edge of a lake, with no parents near at hand, no sponsors at the baptism; springing from nowhere, as Tocqueville had said, standing alone in the presence of God and Nature" (Lewis 104–5).

D. H. Lawrence characterized the *Leatherstocking* novels as "Lovely half-lies" which "form a sort of American Odyssey, with Natty Bumppo for Odysseus": "Only, in the original Odyssey, there is plenty of devil, Circes and swine and all. And Ithacus is devil enough to outwit the devils. But Natty is a saint with a gun, and the Indians are gentlemen through and through, though they may take an occasional scalp" (55). Lawrence's famous summary of the American Odysseus bluntly identifies the dangerous potential of autonomy in the national imaginary: "The essential American soul is hard, isolate, stoic, and a killer" (68).

In many of his nineteenth-century incarnations—which played off earlier constructions of the Boone persona as well as Cooper's Bumppo—Boone became a symbol of frontier violence, imperialist aggression, and even commercial expansion. John A. McClung's *Sketches of Western Adventure* (1832) presents a Boone who is not simply a lover of hunting and wilderness, but of conquest in war with Native Americans. As civilization approaches, "He pined in secret, for the wild and lonely forests of the west—for the immense prairie trodden only by the buffalo, or the elk, and became eager to exchange the listless langor and security of a village, for the healthful exercise of the chase, or the more thrilling excitement of savage warfare" (McClung 85). Slotkin associates Filson's Boone with Jefferson's preference for a contemplative aristocracy, and notes his yielding in the age of Jackson to a more democratic ideal, personified by the "violent, garrulous, slaughter-loving hunter-buffoon, David Crockett" (Slotkin, *Regeneration* 308), who "dwells with great pleasure on the act of killing itself" (415) and finally made "entrepreneurial bear slaughter seem a kind of exalted American profession" (464). In the most famous frontiersmen of the later nineteenth century—from Crockett, to Kit Carson, to Buffalo Bill—the figure darkens considerably, as imperial conquest, and the assertion of white supremacy, become more prominent elements of frontier mythology.

Though the mythic frontiersman reverenced Nature, his sylvan isolation, solitary predation, and antipathy to *nomos* ultimately represent a profound sundering of the eunomic fusion of the political and pastoral. Violent predation forms no significant role in Emerson's or Whitman's conception of autonomy, and is largely sublimated in Thoreau's, but these authors' endorsement of autonomous selfhood augments (in optimistic formulations that swell the self) the nomistic detachment of Boone and Bumppo, and so accelerates eunomic dissolution. But it is in McCarthy's Judge, who preys upon and attempts to contain the entire world, that the autonomy of the mythic frontiersmen will reach its meridian. In him the hunt retains a sacred aura, but only in the sense that Callicles's *physis* suggests the reduction of *themis* to a bare, insentient, agonistic "law of nature" favoring those with Odysseus's polytropic and predatory skills. DeLillo and Shteyngart will give us the endpoint of such autonomy in urban environments, its afterlife or undeath, where ironic "frontiersmen" no longer resist "the multitude," but collapse into it.

4 /   The Deified Self

In all my lectures, I have taught one doctrine, namely, the infinitude of the private man.

—RALPH WALDO EMERSON, *JOURNALS*

Emerson and Thoreau, exceeding the range of Jefferson's skeptical inquiry and intensifying the mythic frontiersman's privileging of solitude within Nature, raise personal autonomy to a kind of ecstatic absoluteness. Turning to the natural world as a tutor for the self, they discover the potential for enormous self-augmentation through disciplined introspection. In contrast, the parochial human conventions of the postrevolutionary American *nomos* are deemed constrictive of the self, and often—and often *intrinsically*—opposed to the themistic order infusing Nature.

Though Emerson and Thoreau each imagine the formation of a new, vitalized nomistic order, they conceive of it as the eventual result of, and subordinate to, the self-pastured person's apotheosis. These authors thus recommence the bifurcative dissolution of eunomia first enacted, but never so exuberantly, in the Greek world. Moreover, in situating the autonomous person at the margins of the actual human *nomos* and investing him with supreme authority to judge that *nomos*, they recast the Socratic *idiotes* in a more seductive and dangerous form. Whereas Socrates's *daemon* was a negative and conservative force, and not at odds with Socrates's civic loyalty, the *daemons* heeded by Emerson and Thoreau offer intoxicating affirmations and exhortations to personal autonomy (the promise, in effect, of an infinitely liberating *enthusiasmos*, or godly possession). This difference licenses an extraordinary growth of the self's scope and powers—effectively deifying it—but also critically weakens communal ties and increases the likelihood of individual pathologies (a dark vulnerability explored, as the conclusion of this chapter briefly illustrates, by Edgar Allan Poe and Herman Melville).

In Walt Whitman we discover a further development of the gigantic, deified self of the Transcendentalists, appearing now within a broader expanse and in more varied shades and detailed contours. Augmenting Emerson and Thoreau—who seem, in comparison, narrowly cerebral and elitist—Whitman celebrates self-pasture's sensual, urban, and democratic potential, while also courting the paradoxical implication of personal autonomy within commercial networks.[1]

Emerson wrote his first significant essay on the classical world, "The Character of Socrates," as a seventeen-year-old at Harvard. Though the work is rather long on praise for the Greek thinker's virtue and short on original insight, it does provide a telling glimpse of what would become guiding ideals in Emerson's maturity. Socrates's great distinction, claims the young scholar, lies in his disregard for mere knowledge and its quotidian uses—the domain of the venal Sophists—and his focus, instead, on deeper psychological truths. Emerson extols Socrates's uncanny mental acuity, his courageous anatomizing of his peers' complacent assumptions as he seeks "to lay open to his own view the human mind, and all its unacknowledged propensities, its weak and fortified positions, and the springs of human action" ("Two Unpublished" 16). Emerson also gives careful consideration to Socrates's fate in opposing "the free tide of an ancient religion," and acknowledges the inveteracy of those holding "old prejudices," who "will repel with indignation the power that came to rend and shatter the whole constitution of [their] soul" (38).

Socrates eventually provided Emerson with a model, in the *daemon* that warned against certain actions, for a universal inner voice. As he notes in an 1828 journal entry: "I suppose that by this Daemon, Socrates designed to describe by a lively image the same judgment which we term conscience. We are all attended by this daemon. We are acquainted with that signal which is as the voice of God" (*Journals* 3:107). In "Plato or, the Philosopher," a chapter in *Representative Men* (1850), Emerson offers a mature reflection on Socrates's extraordinary detachment from material exigencies and conventional social values, and cites in particular his happy poverty, austere self-reliance, invulnerability to alcohol, and physical ugliness. With his nearly magical ability to intuit and expose hidden vulnerabilities in human certainty, Socrates "attacks and brings down all the fine speakers, all the fine philosophers of Athens, whether natives or strangers from Asia Minor and the islands" ("Plato" 437).

By the time he wrote these lines, Emerson had himself been long established, of course, as a speaker and essayist known for attacking conventional authorities. His distinctively *American* contribution, however, was to augment traditional Socratic cross-examination with a new and vigorous affirmation of the private self's infinite depths and powers, claimed by turning to Nature (and away from the human world). And whereas Socrates was resolutely civic-minded, respectful of the benefits conferred by Athens and its laws even as the city martyred him, Emerson, as an American *idiotes* seeking solitary communion with Nature's God, turned inward to find his most binding allegiances. His own daemonic conscience, exuberantly positive in its exhortations, revealed to him a themistic order ultimately underlying and embracing all of humankind, but critically distinct from the human *nomos*. A thoroughgoing irreverence toward nomistic convention is his characteristic stance, and the eunomic fusion of the political and pastoral is critically subordinated in his thought to an ascendant personal autonomy: one journeys toward the divine, best serving oneself and one's community, in solitude. What always trumps the limits and partialities of human convention, Emerson affirms, are the infinite possibilities God makes visible in the nonhuman world. That world corresponds, finally, to the powers of any mind, a point he makes in "The American Scholar" while linking ancient Greece and contemporary America: "'Know thyself' [*gnothi seauton*, the motto inscribed at the Temple of Apollo at Delphi], and the modern precept, 'Study nature,' become at last one maxim" ("American Scholar" 46).

Emerson's first great work, *Nature*, explores the riches of that study. He counsels here a turn to the natural world as a means of stimulating vital, independent thought, and of achieving new intimacies with the divine. Vision is his master metaphor: "Our age," he contends, "is retrospective," and while "forgoing generations beheld God and nature face to face," present-day Americans, belated and purblind, see "through their eyes" (*Nature* 3). The obfuscating lenses of past generations must be removed, so that Americans might achieve—in moments of prophetic insight—a radically disengaged contemplation of "NATURE," which is finally everything that is "NOT ME," "that is, both nature and art, all other men and my own body" (4). Ecstatic vision, Emerson claims, may lead to profound philosophical discoveries (even though they may resist precise expression): "The true philosopher and the true poet are one, and a beauty, which is truth, and a truth, which is beauty, is the aim of both.

Is not the charm of one of Plato's or Aristotle's definitions strictly like that of the Antigone of Sophocles? It is, in both cases, that a spiritual life has been imparted to nature" (29). Emerson's choice of *Antigone* to illustrate his point highlights not just his admiration for the privileging of *themis* over a merely human *nomos*, but his departure from that model in imagining the terms of personal autonomy. The character Antigone is said to have "penetrated the vast masses of nature with an informing soul, and recognized [herself] in their harmony, that is, seized their law" (29), presumably because of her resolute claim to themistic authority (a valiant *auto-nomy* as the self fuses with the law). In an 1835 notebook entry, Emerson lauds her perfect self-containment: "She took up all things into her & in her single self sufficed the soul" (Emerson, *Journals* 5:108). What is most striking in this interpretation is its indifference to Sophocles's fearsome dramatization of Antigone's death, as well as the playwright's balancing of her claim with that of Creon as the representative of *nomos*. The heroine's revelatory insight is all that matters.

The most well-known passage in *Nature*, which recounts one of Emerson's own revelations, still has the power to startle in its description of disembodied containment: "Standing on the bare ground—my head bathed by the blithe air and uplifted into infinite space—all mean egotism vanishes. I become a transparent eyeball; I am nothing; I see all; the currents of the Universal Being circulate through me; I am part or parcel of God" (6). Weirdly and wonderfully, Emerson posits here an apotheosized American self so large it contains the world. Transcendent *intro*spection has canceled and boundlessly augmented the solitary seer: the self becomes "nothing" but still manages both to "see all," and, fusing with the "not me," ultimately be (one with) all. The experience spectacularly exceeds its ancient analogues. It distances the self not just from kinship networks, but from any affective connections with others as the entire nomistic world falls away during a moment of rapturous self-pasture: "The name of the nearest friend sounds then foreign and accidental: to be brothers, to be acquaintances, master or servant, is then a trifle and a disturbance" (6). The detachment attained is much more extreme than Socrates's trance-like contemplations of abstract truth (see *Symposium*, 175 B, 220 C–D), for it posits, in place of the Athenian's typically circumspect claims about any knowledge of the divine, an audacious assertion of the self's unlimited themistic potency. Similarly, whereas Antigone commits herself to a particular, external, and fixed divine law, Emerson's fusion with the divine implies a radically internalized and fluid self-pasture. Moreover, the effectively infinite dimensions of personal autonomy encountered here dramatically surpass those implied by Jefferson's vision at the Natural Bridge, Natty Bumppo's christening as "Hawkeye," or any sylvan epiphany attributed to Daniel Boone. They also anticipate, as we shall see, the ecstatic (and catastrophic) "natural" liberation of McCarthy's Judge—a warrior more single-minded than any major character in Homeric myth, who carries out an apocalyptic quest for the annihilation of all that is "not me"—as well as the self-consumptive pasturing of DeLillo and Shteyngart's hyperautonomists.

In beholding and merging with infinite themistic prospects, Emerson casts the natural world, finally, as an utterly obliging medium through which the divine might be known and the self remade. The *auto-nomia* of that self implies the most positive senses of the Greek verb *nemo*, a richly sustaining self-possession and self-inhabitance. Simultaneously, Emerson's vision entails an ultimate and paradoxical diminution of *themis* in the face of the augmented self and its freedom to range and possess what lies before it. In his description of how Nature lies waiting to be subordinated to personal will, he employs figurative language that suggests, perhaps jarringly for contemporary readers, a sort of commercial enterprise undertaken by a world-beating colonist adventuring in God's name: "Nature is thoroughly mediate. It is made to serve. It receives the dominion of man as meekly as the ass on which the Savior rode. It offers all its kingdoms to man as the raw material which he may mold into what is useful" (*Nature* 21). Emerson turns the conclusion of *Nature* over to his "poet," an exuberantly affirmative "inner voice" that promises new prospects for all visionaries: "'Build therefore your own world. As fast as you can conform your life to the pure idea in your mind, that will unfold its great proportions'" (*Nature* 39). Any ambitious prospector, Emerson would suggest, might claim kingdoms and their raw materials, given that the natural world is not just compliant but democratically receptive: each self may discover and graze upon an infinite and infinitely fertile private pasture. Though Emerson's emphasis falls, clearly, on affirming the *conceptual* possibilities of Nature's resources, the practical application of one's dominion over them seems to follow. As Myra Jehlen notes, his limitless vision "naturally" finds a counterpart in "unchecked entrepreneurial development" (Jehlen 100). That development will suggest, amid the emergence of personal hyperautonomy in the late twentieth and early twenty-first centuries, an unsustainable self-pasture and Nature's (perhaps imminent) exhaustibility.

"Self-Reliance," the essay for which Emerson is perhaps best known, furnishes the most direct celebrations of personal autonomy, and elaborates the intoxicating creed of the American *idiotes*. Self-reliance depends, he insists, on trusting one's own intuition, and on applying it in one's judgments of others: "To believe your own thought, to believe that what is true for you in your private heart is true for all men—that is genius" (132). Social coercion was, as the historian Gordon S. Wood explains, a formidable reality for early-nineteenth-century Americans: "This vast, impersonal, and democratic idea of public opinion soon came to dominate all of American intellectual life. In all endeavors— whether art, language, medicine, or politics—connoisseurs, professors, doctors, and statesmen had to give way before the power of the collective opinion of the people" (Wood 312). That power, Emerson affirms in his neo-Socratic defense of the private self's themistic insight against nomistic convention, is resolutely aligned against the *idiotes*—producing what Lord Byron called, in his paean to Daniel Boone, "the dwarfing city's pale abortions" (*Don Juan* 8.66), or what Mailer will diagnose as the "conformity and depression," the "stench of fear [. . . coming out] of every pore of American life" ("White Negro" 312). Communal voices threaten to drown out the wisdom any individual might hear, and so bar him from realizing his potential: "Society everywhere is in conspiracy against the manhood of every one of its members" ("Self-Reliance" 134).

Socrates's refusal to flee the death sentence Athens imposed on him, and his insistence that the citizen is profoundly indebted to (and morally "fenced in" by) the *nomos* which nurtured him (see *Crito* 51 D–E) provide a telling contrast to Emerson's exuberant endorsements of the American *idiotes*' ultimate freedom to range. Emersonian autonomy derogates the actual nomistic world in centering the self upon itself: "Let us affront and reprimand the smooth mediocrity and squalid contentment of the times, and hurl in the face of custom and trade and office, the fact which is the upshot of all history, that there is a great responsible Thinker and Actor working wherever a man works" ("Self-Reliance" 139–40). At his most hyperbolic, Emerson seems, for a gentle scholar, oddly redolent of Callicles, deriding *nomos* as nothing more than illusory restraint, and taking *physis*—the "natural" process favoring the strong over the weak—as the bare reality of themistic order: "We do not yet see that virtue is Height, and that a man or a company of men, plastic and permeable to principles, by the law of nature must overpower and ride all cities, nations, kings, rich men, poets, who are not" (144). And again: "Power is, in nature, the essential measure of right" (144). In McCarthy's Judge, Emerson's Calliclean sympathies are combined with the frontiersman's predatory ethos and extended to an endpoint that both absorbs and *empties* the world.

It is, seemingly, the task of the American *idiotes* to reject a corrupt *nomos* in search of personal autonomy, to listen for and respond to the authentic voice of Nature's God. In Emerson's reckoning, what makes this task *un*-Calliclean is God's ultimate benignity; what protects it from mere self-indulgence is the great courage and discipline required to hear divinity in Nature and heed the demands it makes on the self. There is, he makes clear, formidable labor involved in the cultivation of autonomy (the inadequacy of "individualism" as a description of what is involved here should stand out): "And truly it commands something godlike in him who has cast off the common motives of humanity and has ventured to trust himself for a taskmaster. High be his heart, faithful his will, clear his sight, that he may in good earnest be doctrine, society, law, to himself, that a simple purpose may be to him as strong as iron necessity is to others!" (146). Emerson's core faith—and American autonomy's core vulnerability— is that in becoming a "law unto oneself," self-shepherding one's private pasture, one will discover an ennobling, unifying, and finally *self-less* common ground with other selves.

In "The Over-Soul," Emerson sets out the final unity of all selves within such privacy, emphasizing not aggressive self-assertion but submission: "Meantime within man is the soul of the whole; the wise silence; the universal beauty, to which every part and particle is equally related; the eternal ONE. And this deep power in which we exist, and whose beatitude is all accessible to us, is not only self-sufficing and perfect in every hour, but the act of seeing and the thing seen, the seer and the spectacle, the subject and the object, are one" ("Over-Soul" 237). This is the shared space in which Emerson, as a representative seer, achieves his transcendence: Nature's universality promises not isolation and emptiness, at last, but a democratic plenitude. Lawrence Buell explains Emerson's conviction about the ends of self-reliance: "The Me at the bottom of the me, the 'Trustee' or 'aboriginal Self' on which reliance may be safely grounded, is despite whatever appearances to the contrary not a merely personal interest or entity but a universal. The more inward you go, the less individuated you get. Beneath and within the 'private' is a 'public' power on which anyone can potentially draw. So Self-Reliance involves not a single but a double negative: resistance to external pressure, then resistance to shallow impulse" (Buell 65). Self-reliance, for Emerson, may devalue the nomistic world, but it does not finally isolate the autonomous person from his community. The *idiotes* may produce, as Buell puts it, "ripple effects" on the polis, even though "the chief focus of his interest . . . always remains mental emancipation at the individual level. 'Mental self-reliance' is 'the *model* of active self-reliance'" (67). Emerson's faith was that these ripple effects would invigorate rather than dissipate the polis, that inward journeying would produce outward revitalization, and so reassert themistic order in the corrupted human *nomos*.

Thoreau explores the concrete, practical expression of autonomy much more directly and precisely than his mentor Emerson, while also sketching the contours of political "ripples" and their potential to transform the nomistic world as disruptive waves (in his concern for the particular and pragmatic, he plays the role, we might say, of the empiricist Aristotle to Emerson's idealist Plato). A sort of frontier *idiotes*, Thoreau combines nomistic critique with immersion in, and the personal cultivation of, natural "wildness." He provides not just a record of his actual experiments in living a self-reliant, examined life, close to Nature's God, but elaborates an ethics of the inner voice and sets forth a rationale for the autonomous person's justified revolt against nomistic authorities.

Settling in to his cabin at Walden Pond on July 4, 1845, Thoreau gave his retreat an ancient frame: "My house makes me think of some mountain houses I have seen, which seemed to have a fresher auroral atmosphere about them, as I fancy of the halls of Olympus. . . . I am glad to remember to-night, as I sit by my door, that I too am at least a remote descendent of that heroic race of men of whom there is tradition. I too sit here on the shore of my Ithaca, a fellow-wanderer and survivor of Ulysses" (*Writings* 7:361, 363). Allusions to Greek mythology are scattered throughout *Walden*, and Thoreau clearly saw himself as recuperating some of the vitality he associated with the ancient world. The Greeks' liberty, in the idealized form he ascribed to it, had both negative and positive virtues: freedom *from* the tyranny of mechanical timepieces, the "quiet desperation" of industrialized labor, and the coercions of trivial modern entertainments, along with the freedom *to* commune with the untamed representatives of *themis* populating the nonhuman environment. In the American woods, he would escape the "greater part of what my neighbors call good" (*Walden* 11), heeding the *daemon* offering, as for Emerson, affirmative and self-liberating rather than merely cautionary counsel: "I hear an irresistible voice which invites me away from all that" (11). Where Jefferson's ideal was a community of yeoman farmers, Thoreau shrinks the pastoral unit to one (and all) as he heeds the daemonic invitation.

Sole governor of his small cabin and garden, Thoreau conducts in *Walden* a scrupulous accounting of his personal "economy"—the self-constructed "home-law/pasture" of his private *oikos* (household)—and attempts, as part of the cultivation of a sort of field-tested autonomy, to work out his authentic obligations to himself and his community. He practices a profound skepticism toward received opinion, but in contrast to the Socratic dialogues, his version of *elenchus* does not, typically, involve the intimate, one-on-one interrogation of an interlocutor represented as physically present and able to answer in his own voice. Instead, the text assumes the self's physical separation from others as a necessary starting point for a contemplation of the claims of *nomos* and *themis*, and thus resembles something like a record of the self's communion with itself (as, once again, all). The goal here is to escape a stupefying conformity of thought and so wake, continuously, to new and vital worlds, the fertile pastures of the self which, for the mass of men, are barricaded or blighted by the nomistic world. "[Be] a Columbus," Thoreau advises, "to whole new continents and worlds within you, opening new channels, not of trade, but of thought" (258).

Like Emerson, Thoreau records ecstatic moments in which he seems to merge with Nature's God. Affective human allegiances temporarily drop away for the sylvan explorer at the realization of "such sweet and beneficent society in Nature": "Every little pine needle expanded and swelled with sympathy and befriended me. I was so distinctly aware of the presence of something kindred to me, even in scenes which we are accustomed to call wild and dreary, and also that the nearest of blood to me and humanest was not a person nor a villager, that I thought no place could ever be strange to me again" (107). In another such moment—often compared to Emerson's transparent eyeball passage, but achieved, in a telling difference, through *active* labor—Thoreau both loses his nomistic and finds his themistic selfhood. Hoeing in his bean field, he convenes, contains, and then forgets other humans, past and present, disappearing into his work while expanding infinitely in identification with the natural world: "When my hoe tinkled against the stones, that music echoed to the woods and the sky, and was an accompaniment to my labor which yielded an instant and immeasurable crop. It was no longer beans that I hoed nor I that hoed beans; and I remembered with as much pity as pride, if I remembered at all, my acquaintances who had gone to the city to attend the oratorios" (129). The self finds, once again, a nourishing infinitude within as it leaves behind its nomistic bonds.

Such moments emerge organically out of, and in turn inform the practice of, an active engagement with the natural world. Laboring in his garden or wandering through the forest, Thoreau confronts and is augmented by the infinite potency of the "not me." Encounters with Nature's fecundity and ferocity stimulate the self's assumption of its own powers: "We must be refreshed by the sight of inexhaustible vigor, vast and titanic features, the sea-coast with its wrecks, the wilderness with its living and its decaying trees, the thunder-cloud, and the rain which lasts three weeks and produces freshets. We need to witness our own limits transgressed, and some life pasturing freely where we never wander" (255). The "tonic of wildness" (255) *stretches* the self (from the Greek *tonikos*, "of or for stretching"), pulls it away from and keeps it in a state of dynamic tension with both personal and social complacencies. Such tension defines an autonomy doubly allied with the spiritual and the animalistic, which balances the claims of human and natural worlds. Within that fertile self-pasture, Thoreau aims, like Epicurus, to identify and savor the most profound, reliable, lasting pleasures. Much of *Walden* is, in fact, dedicated to the senses, which become a conduit for the divine (though never quite in the eroticized and unrestrainedly manic mode of Whitman). Whereas Emerson *lost* his corporeality in becoming a "transparent eyeball," Thoreau recoups it, and is thus able to enjoy "delicious evening[s] . . . when the whole body is one sense, and imbibes delight through every pore" (105). Not simple sensuous indulgence, but a complex, disciplined economy of the senses is pursued here, guided by a tonic asceticism. Thoreau claims water to be "the only wise drink for a wise man," and derides wine, coffee, and tea, along with *music*, as dangerous intoxicants: "Ah, how low I fall when I am tempted by them! Even music may be intoxicating. Such apparently slight causes destroyed Greece and Rome, and will destroy England and America" (175). Ideally, the self is, for Thoreau, stretched between bestial voracity and angelic meditation, and he aims to "reverence them both," for he "[loves] the wild not less than the good" (170). In "Walking," he imagines himself moving profitably and continually, in the tonic fashion described above, between the civilized and primitive worlds: "For my part, I feel that with regard to Nature I live a sort of border life, on the confines of a world into which I make occasional and transient forays only, and my patriotism and allegiance to the state into whose territories I seem to retreat are those of a moss-trooper" (777). Thoreau might have said "frontiersman" instead of "moss-trooper"—the latter refers to seventeenth-century marauders who periodically crossed the mosses of the Scottish border—for his active ideal is similar to Boone's or Bumppo's, lacking a personal readiness for violence, certainly, but with a certain restless aggression, a coiled wildness, preserved within it.

Though Thoreau sees individual isolation as the starting point for the cultivation of autonomy, and can at times seem (in spite of his denials) inveterately hostile to communal life and even misanthropic, he conceived of his experiment at Walden Pond not as a permanent escape from *nomos* and political responsibility, but as a means of personal maturation that might have communal benefits. He remains committed, we might say, to the eunomic fusion of the pastoral and political—holding *ten*-uously to it, perhaps, but holding still. In this sense, then, he is un-Epicurean, for he casts himself as ultimately oriented toward making his audience, and his *nomos* generally, more vital and just: where Socrates played the role of gadfly to the sluggish, he will be a "chanticleer" to the wildness in the slumbering masses. Stanley Cavell rightly notes that while *Walden* demonstrates that "education for citizenship is education for isolation," the book is nevertheless "a tract of political education, education for membership in the polis. It locates authority in the citizens and it identifies citizens—those with whom one is in membership—as 'neighbors'" (Cavell 85).

How, exactly, political engagement might look is worked out more precisely in Thoreau's political essays, which characteristically echo Antigone's reverence for themistic over nomistic authority. "Civil Disobedience"[2] begins by boldly invoking and extending a formula for liberty associated with Jefferson: "I heartily accept the motto,—'That government is best which governs least;' and I should like to see it acted up to more rapidly and systematically. Carried out, it finally amounts to this, which also I believe,—'That government is best which governs not at all;' and when men are prepared for it, that will be the kind of government which they will have" ("Civil" 729). It is, Thoreau makes clear, a call for *better* (rather than no) government that he is making, but his essential endorsement is of maximal personal autonomy. Since bad government *does* exist in the present moment, autonomous persons may find themselves in direct conflict with their *nomos*, but if so, they should not hesitate to rebel: if you are "[required] to be the agent of injustice to another, then, I say, break the law" (737). What is it, then, that guides one's self-pasture? Conscience, insists Thoreau, reflects a supreme themistic authority, a "higher law," against which the legitimacy of any *nomos* may be judged. For Thoreau, as for Emerson, a benignant divinity speaks through the natural world. Obedience to "the law of nature" sanctions compassionate treatment of others—hence the basis for opposing slavery and imperial warfare—and promotes the flourishing of all autonomous persons. No mere "individualism" is involved here, Thoreau asserts, in the self's radical commitment to themistic authority: "Action from principle—the perception and the performance of right—changes things and relations; it is essentially revolutionary, and does not consist wholly with anything which was. It not only divides states and churches, it divides families; ay, it divides the *individual*, separating the diabolical in him from the divine" (736).

More rugged assessments of civil disobedience—which authorize *active* resistance to government injustice—emerge from Thoreau's later essays on slavery. The authority to act is grounded firmly in the individual conscience. No matter what any Founding Father might have decreed, there is, Thoreau argues in "Slavery in Massachusetts," no legitimate law but that which one finds (in the divinity) within, "the eternal and only just CONSTITUTION which He, and not any Jefferson or Adams, has written into your being" ("Slavery" 868). If a human law shadows and blasphemes God's gift of inner light, then action in defiance of tyranny is justified in the defense of natural rights. In "A Plea for Captain John Brown," an apology for the abolitionist leader of the Pottawatomie Massacre of 1856 and raid at Harpers Ferry in 1859, Thoreau elaborates his validation of rebellion against the state, and counters the pacifism associated with "Civil Disobedience" with an apparent sanctioning of violence in the service of emancipatory ends. The legitimacy of any action depends, Thoreau argues, on personal reckoning, regardless of whatever nomistic restriction might be set against it: "Any man knows when he is justified, and all the wits in the world cannot enlighten him on that point. . . . I do not believe in lawyers, in that mode of attacking or defending a man, because you descend to meet the judge on his own ground, and, in cases of the highest importance, it is of no consequence whether a man breaks a human law or not" ("A Plea" 941–42). Thoreau's stance here mirrors that of Antigone, but adds an apparent willingness to act violently, when occasion demands it, against the state. The autonomous American owes nothing to *nomos*, and may feel justified in striking out against it when its claims conflict with those of the themistic authority within.

The detached perspective on human communities endorsed by Thoreau, along with the cultivation of an active "wildness" and the license to "break the law," are framed much more darkly by Poe and Melville, as well as the twentieth- and twenty-first-century authors explored in this study. In them we discover the inherent perils, for individual and community alike, of the self's nomistic detachment, and a vivid range of pathological possibilities generated amid eunomic dissolution.

Thoreau's championing of sensuous life, as we have seen, was carefully balanced with a tonic restraint that can ultimately seem ascetic (and even, so far as *sensual* experience goes, severely and strangely prudish). In Whitman's work, however, we encounter a kind of Dionysian explosion of the senses, an unrestrained delight in the deified self's corporeal, eroticized potential. Offering his own experience as a democratic model, Whitman finally locates that potential within urban settings—a startling development when we consider the American emphasis, from Jefferson through the mythic frontiersman to the Transcendentalists, on Nature's God actually residing in the natural world. Fusing *themis* with the urban *nomos*, he celebrates a kind of *urbs naturae*, a city of nature.

In *Leaves of Grass*, Whitman embraces a fusion of self and world analogous to that described by Emerson and Thoreau: "With time and space I him dilate and fuse the immortal laws, / To make himself by them the law unto himself" ("For Him I Sing" lines 4–5). But where Emerson's "transparent eyeball" would restrict the self's deification to a disembodied *visionary* experience, and Thoreau's to a broader but still strictly limited sensuous receptivity, in Whitman all the senses proffer an unbridled themistic potency: "Divine am I inside and out, and I make holy whatever I / touch or am touch'd from, / The scent of these arm-pits aroma finer than prayer, / This head more than churches, bibles, and all the creeds" ("Song of Myself" lines 524–26). The body becomes yet another expression of, and a means of merging with, Nature's God, and erotic imperatives are reinterpreted as part of the self's holiness. The phallus is venerated, in an astonishing image linking body and land, as the great cultivator of the self's pasture:

> If I worship one thing more than another it shall be the spread of
> my own body, or any part of it,
> Translucent mould of me it shall be you!
> Shaded ledges and rests it shall be you!
> Firm masculine colter it shall be you!
> Whatever goes to the tilth of me it shall be you! (lines 527–31)

A broader receptivity to instinct, to the self's spontaneous imperatives, would negate nomistic hostility to the flesh—for Whitman, the great lingering curse of Puritanism and the Christian *themis*—and dramatically enlarge possibilities for (deified) self-expression.

Whitman's physicality and eroticism famously troubled Thoreau, who balanced his praise of *Leaves* with reservations about its "simply sensual" exhortations, suggestive to him of something subhuman, a yielding to a version of *physis* excluding any transcendence: "[Whitman] does not celebrate love at all. It is as if the beasts spoke. I think that men have not been ashamed of themselves without reason. No doubt there have always been dens where such deeds were unblushingly recited, and it is no merit to compete with their inhabitants. But even on this side he has spoken more truth than any American or modern that I know. I have found his poem exhilarating, encouraging" (Thoreau, *Writings* 295–96). In later chapters, we shall see how Mailer's outlaws seek to reclaim a bestial (and ostensibly vivifying) sensuality in defiance of lingering Puritanical inhibitions, whereas DeLillo and Shteyngart's hyperautonomists encounter (typically) a disinhibited and disorienting wonderland of eroticized self-pasture.

The sacred body is worshipped most "naturally," Whitman implies, by simple folk, and as part of his strategy of universal containment he includes descriptions of a number of representative pastoral figures, wholesome in their separateness from urban spaces. We encounter, for instance, an idealized "common farmer" ("I Sing the Body Electric" line 33), a contemporary version of Jefferson's "chosen people of God": "When he went with his five sons and many grand-sons to / hunt or fish, you would pick him out as the most / beautiful and vigorous of the gang, / You would wish long and long to be with him, you would / wish to sit by him in the boat that you and he might / touch each other" (lines 43–44). Frontier mythology is also saluted, in markedly clichéd terms, along with a blending, blessed by Nature, of "red" and "white":

> Alone far in the wilds and mountains I hunt,
> Wandering amazed at my own lightness and glee,
> In the late afternoon choosing a safe spot to pass the night,
> Kindling a fire and broiling the fresh-kill'd game,
> Falling asleep on the gather'd leaves with my dog and gun by my
> side.
>
> . . . .
>
> I saw the marriage of the trapper in the open air in the far west, the
> bride was a red girl . . . ("Song of Myself" lines 175–79, 185)

Along with such conventional pastoralism, *Leaves of Grass* includes, however, a number of (usually much more innovative and startling) explorations of city life. These passages reverse the pastoral emphasis so crucial to the American discovery of Nature's God as they reveal, within urban spaces, a divinity matching anything in the natural world. In stark contrast to Jefferson, Boone, Bumppo, Emerson, and Thoreau, whose preference is for communing with the divine outside the "city's pale abortions," here the urban world (and everything else) is divinely blessed pasture:

> Thrive, cities—bring your freight, bring your shows, ample and
>   sufficient rivers,
> Expand, being than which none else is perhaps more spiritual,
> Keep your places, objects than which none else is more lasting.
> ("Crossing Brooklyn Ferry" lines 123–25)

Urban scenes function like "natural" ones: Whitman's speaker is stimulated, like Jefferson, by their potency; he pioneers their "settlement," like Boone and Bumppo; he enthusiastically fuses himself with all he encounters, like Emerson and Thoreau. Rejecting inherited nomistic restrictions, he reconstructs the human *nomos* as, paradoxically, a projection of the deified self. Having laid full claim to *themis* and forged a potent personal autonomy (one that is, in its endless identifications with others, profoundly and intrinsically hypersocial), the self may range at will from polis to polis:

> Afoot and light-hearted I take to the open road,
> Healthy, free, the world before me,
> The long brown path before me leading wherever I choose.
> . . . .
> From this hour I ordain myself loos'd of limits and imaginary lines,
> Going where I list, my own master total and absolute,
> Listening to others, considering well what they say,
> Pausing, searching, receiving, contemplating,
> Gently, but with undeniable will, divesting myself of the holds that
>   would hold me.
> I inhale great draughts of space,
> The east and the west are mine, and the north and the south are
>   mine. ("Song of the Open Road" lines 1–3, 53–59)

One's self-pasture, on these terms, is inexhaustible: "To see no possession but you may possess it, enjoying all / without labor or purchase, abstracting the feast yet not / abstracting one particle of it" (line 174). It is as if polytropic Odysseus absorbed the gods and journeyed everywhere, "seeing the cities and knowing the minds of men," yet always found himself feasting at home.

Such autonomy is, Whitman insists, for everyone. Though the self may claim all, all may claim such a self: "I will accept nothing which all cannot have their / counterpart of on the same terms" ("Song of Myself" line 507). Every American, he prophesied in his preface to the 1855 edition of *Leaves*, will soon shepherd his own pasture: "A new order shall arise and they shall be the priests of man, and every man shall be his own priest. . . . Through the divinity of themselves shall the kosmos and the new breed of poets be interpreters of men and women and of all events and things" (760). Usurping all external religious authority, Whitman affirms—like Emerson and Thoreau, but much more brazenly—the self's indwelling divinity, utterly self-sufficient and yet linked to other selves: "And nothing, not God, is greater to one than one's self is, / And whoever walks a furlong without sympathy walks to / his own funeral drest in his shroud" ("Song of Myself" lines 1271–72).

Personal autonomy, Whitman makes clear, seeks a comprehensive absorption, a heroic containment of diversity that will function as a model of any individual's creative power. This achievement comes not by standing apart from the crowd—as in the figure of the isolated Romantic, unreconciled to the world—but by joining and celebrating the mass. Whitman's poetic stance is fundamentally democratic: "The messages of great poets to each man and woman are, Come to us on equal terms, Only then can you understand us, We are no better than you, What we enclose you enclose, What we enjoy you may enjoy" ("Leaves of Grass, 1855" line 750). The subjects of poetry are thus made commensurate with the poet himself: mere existence makes one the equal of whomever would record one's life in art. Poetic self-pasturing involves a kind of dynamic mimicry—"Only toward as good as itself and toward the like of itself will [the soul of the nation] advance half-way" (762)—and mass approval certifies its ultimate achievement: "The proof of a poet is that his country absorbs him as affectionately as he has absorbed it" (762). The urban and democratic emphasis of Whitman's self-pasture thus returns personal autonomy—in a critical paradox—to crowds and commercial networks: that is, to precisely those things from which Jefferson sought to remove himself, and Boone and Bumppo finally could not. When Whitman announces "I celebrate myself" ("Song of Myself" line 1), his choice of verb could not be more telling. What he seeks as a poet is to *make* his renown, to produce it artificially, to create what the Romans called *celebritas*. The achievement of such renown is no longer associated with the gods (understood externally), for he contains them and takes on their role as artificer: he need not wait for fame (the Greeks' *pheme* or the Romans' *fama*), emerging and spreading organically, mysteriously, uncontrollably. He will generate his renown himself, manipulate it, commodify it within nomistic structures (while yet standing apart from them, autonomously, as a deified self which projects its own human *nomos*).

Whitman may seem here, in identifying the self with the masses, to have reconstituted ancient Greek *eunomia* in his *urbs naturae*. However, what is radically new is the boundless *auto*nomy of that fusion: the nomistic world here is not, as it was for the early Greeks, a dimension of the themistic one, which places and subordinates the self within a larger order external to the human will, but is, instead, a projection of order and universal sympathy *out of* the deified self. Mailer's work will chart the pathologies and lurid (if, for him, potentially still vital) reclamations of urban autonomy, while DeLillo and Shteyngart's novels illustrate fully, in the figure of the hyperautonomist, the utter implication of the deified self within commercial networks, amounting to a sterile, masturbatory self-possession that finally strips Whitman's erotic containment of profound social (or even extrapersonal) bonds.

Emerson, Thoreau, and Whitman's valorization of personal autonomy, linked for each with hopes for a revitalized polis, licenses the self to remake the world. Poe and Melville investigate the vulnerability of a faith in the self's privacy, generating a sort of shadow play on the Transcendentalists' optimism, which represents, as a new and incipient phenomenon, the forbidding personal and social consequences of eunomic dissolution. Poe's sickly inward adventurers, and Melville's imperial Ahab and Colonel John Moredock, along with his shape-shifting Confidence-Man, bring forth the destructive senses of the Greek verb *nemo*: a possession and inhabitation suggestive of ulcerous spreading and fiery consumption.

Go inward, implies Poe, and you may indeed find infinitude—but it is likely to be fog-ridden, festering, torturous, at last self-annihilating. The faith informing Jefferson's and the Transcendentalists' *themis* undergoes a decisive change here; one discovers no benignant Nature that might nourish the autonomous person and a revivified *nomos*, but rather a lurking malevolence and intimations of supernatural perfidy. Without the helpful guidance of the natural world or assurances that an Oversoul binds humankind, the self—now thoroughly detached from its *nomos*—begins to feed *on* itself, and becomes a persecuted and power-less judge of, and threat to, the nomistic world from which it is isolated. Mental spaces become febrile and claustrophobic; physical space often shrinks drastically. The walled-in tombs and live burials that recur in Poe's work with obsessive frequency—chilling (and telling) variations on Antigone's fate—illustrate a terminally centripetal self-pasture.[3] Mental and physical spaces tend, in fact, to blur, and their exploration reveals, as William Wilson discovers (here speaking from the innocence of youth, before his encounter with self-estrangement has begun to overwhelm him), a disorienting boundlessness:

> But the house!—how quaint an old building was this!—to me how veritably a palace of enchantment! There was really no end to its windings—to its incomprehensible subdivisions. It was difficult, at any given time, to say with certainty upon which of its two stories one happened to be. From each room to every other there were sure to be found three or four steps either in ascent or descent. Then the lateral branches were innumerable—inconceivable—and so return-ing in upon themselves, that our most exact ideas in regard to the whole mansion were not very far different from those with which we pondered upon infinity. ("William Wilson" 219)

The private *daemons* accessed by Poe's characters typically counsel impulsive release, mad action, murder, and the *outward* expression of inward journeying becomes, most characteristically, a brutal and futile catharsis. The self erupts in civil war: "Who has not, a hundred times, found himself committing a vile or a silly action, for no other reason than because he knows he should *not*? . . . It was this unfathomable long-ing of the soul *to vex itself*—to offer violence to its own nature—to do wrong for the wrong's sake only—that urged me to continue and finally to consummate the injury I had inflicted upon the unfortunate brute" ("The Black Cat" 350; italics in original).

Poe's short tale "The Man of the Crowd" presents the city itself as the breeding ground of a pathological self-pasture, and thus prolepti-cally refutes Whitman's urban optimism, as well as prefigures DeLillo's hyperautonomists, whose inward journeying leads back to a volatile predation on the "mass of men" and the nomistic world. Absorbed in watching and categorizing the crowds who walk by him, the tale's nar-rator reduces individuals to types. Crowds do not suggest democratic vitality here, as they do for Whitman, but internal wastes: one subject of the narrator's gaze is judged to be an "unequivocal beauty in the prime of her womanhood, putting one in mind of the statue in Lucian, with the surface of Parian marble, and the interior filled with filth" (234–35). At last fixing on a peculiar, uncategorizable man who dashes among the denizens of the street, the narrator follows him through the slums of the teeming metropolis and comes to understand—in what seems in part a self-revelation—the man's awareness of an interior wasteland, the terror of his dark private self driving him to seek company: "'This old man,' I said at length, 'is the type and the genius of deep crime. He refuses to be alone. *He is the man of the crowd*" (239).

Private revelations have, in this blighted *urbs naturae*, the quality of an affliction. "Conscience" offers no reassuring guidance—"Now and then, alas, the conscience of man takes up a burden so heavy in horror that it can be thrown down only into the grave. And thus the essence of all crime is undivulged" (232)—and visionary insight hints at violence: "For some months I had been ill in health, but was now convalescent, and, with returning strength, found myself in one of those happy moods which are so precisely the converse of *ennui*—moods of the keenest appetency, when the film from the mental vision departs—the αχλυς ος πριν επηεν—and the intellect, electrified, surpasses as greatly its every-day condition, as does the vivid yet candid reason of Leibnitz, the mad and flimsy rhetoric of Gorgias" (232). The Greek words—"the mist formerly upon [your eyes]"—are spoken by Athene in book 5 of the *Iliad* as she promises to grant Diomedes, who has just appealed to her for assistance in battle, the ability to distinguish gods and men.[4] A mass slaughter follows, with a vividly antipastoral bent:

> Though he had been eager to do battle with the Trojans before, now he was seized with a fury three times as strong. He acts as a lion who has leapt over the wall of a pen, and who is wounded but not killed by a shepherd in the field tending to his wooly sheep. His strength is summoned, and the shepherd defends himself no more, instead retreating to his farmhouse. The flock is left completely undefended, is torn apart, and the sheep are thrown together, each of them piled on one another, before the furious lion leaps forth again across the wall. It is with such fury that the powerful Diomedes joined the Trojans. (*Iliad* 5.133–65)

In the Homeric world, this is grand heroism, an instance of *aristeia* ("excellence") in which the warrior fulfils, even exceeds with the help of divine assistance, his human potential in armed combat. Emerson's and Thoreau's moments of sublime, rapturous self-pasture might be thought of as the Transcendental versions of *aristeia*, involving a god-fuelled "victory" of the autonomous person over the nomistic world. For Poe's narrator, however, the moment of *aristeia* suggests a sort of themistic derangement, an occult *enthusiasm* (possession by a god suggesting here the negative sense of *nemo* as ulcerous spread) threatening horrific expression in an incongruous field.

In Captain Ahab, Melville presents another enthusiastic automatist, here in a titanic form that sweeps along a group of others to destruction. Like the Transcendentalists, Ahab sees a themistic authority beyond the "signs" of the natural world—"All visible objects, man, are but as pasteboard masks" (*Moby Dick* 178)—but for him they signify a mischievous and malevolent power, an ultimate spiritual reality suggestive of "an inscrutable malice" (178) (a vision of *physis* as, effectively, something like the bleakest remnant of *themis*). "All evil" is "visibly personified" in Moby Dick, Nature's most fitting representative, here not at all Emersonian— "thoroughly mediate" and "made to serve"—but fatally opposed to the "dominion of man" (Emerson, *Nature* 21). Personal autonomy becomes paradoxically self-annihilating in Ahab's doomed agon with Nature's God, for the ferocious austerity of his willfulness reduces *him* to nothing more than a malevolent mask—a monomaniacal, self-consumed law unto himself. Caught in a terminal vortex like the *Pequod* at the novel's end, he is all but eliminated *as* a self.

A landlubberly counterpart to Ahab can be found in the figure of "the late Colonel John Moredock," who is discussed by various interlocutors aboard a ship called the *Fidèle* in *The Confidence-Man: His Masquerade* (1857). An actual historical figure said here to have "hated Indians like snakes'" (187) and to have earned "Terror' [as] his epitaph" (200), Moredock anticipates McCarthy's Judge in having converted the frontiersman's sacred hunt to serial slaughter. Though reminiscent of the Transcendentalists in his cultivation of self-law—"he must depend upon himself; he must continually look to himself. Hence self-reliance, to the degree of standing by his own judgment, though it stand alone" (193)—*his* autonomy is cut off from conventional (nomistic) piety: "Like the 'possum, the backwoodsman presents the spectacle of a creature dwelling exclusively among the works of God, yet these, truth must confess, breed little in him of a godly mind" (193). All the rugged skills associated with the frontiersman are turned in Moredock to the pursuit of private vengeance (his relatives have apparently been killed by Native Americans), making him, like Ahab, something like the personification of a privately focalized rage: "Master of that woodland cunning enabling the adept to subsist where the tyro would perish, and expert in all those arts by which an enemy is pursued for weeks, perhaps months, without once suspecting it, he kept to the forest. The solitary Indian that met him, died. When a number was descried, he would either secretly pursue their track for some chance to strike at least one blow; or if, while thus engaged, he himself was discovered, he would elude them by superior skill" (205–6). Moredock is associated, in fact, with a distinctively American commitment to violence, one that exceeds all classical precedents: "Though, like suicide, man-hatred would seem peculiarly a Roman and a Grecian passion—that is, pagan; yet, the annals of neither Rome nor Greece can produce the equal in man-hatred of Colonel Moredock" (210).

The other passengers aboard the *Fidèle* do not possess Moredock's viciousness, yet they, too, suggest pathological forms of autonomy. Self-conscious role players, they seemingly disguise themselves (or the absence of any self) behind carefully crafted personae. Though set aboard a riverboat, Melville's novel represents the alienated conditions of urban life and cosmopolitan mixing, in which strangers are thrown together and must puzzle out, amid much gamesmanship, the trustworthiness of each other's social masks. The novel's Confidence-Man (or men, for his plurality is precisely the point) is the representative figure, and he demonstrates a self-delighting polytropism akin to—though, in its democratized American form, much more trivial than—that of Odysseus. The interiority of such a figure disappears into its outward performances, reversing the dynamic of Emersonian autonomy. As Gary Lindberg summarizes the key transition: "Emerson postulates a being who can exist quite independent of social relations; Melville counters with an agent who exists only in the mutability of those relations" (Lindberg 43). Tony Tanner sees the Confidence-Man, in fact, as a kind of American Socrates, performing a version of *elenchus* that strips confidence in the stability of any self: "[he] does indeed initiate a series of latter-day Platonic dialogues with himself . . . [so that his] various interlocutors are forced (or persuaded), in one way or another, to reveal themselves, or, better, they are variously unmasked, though whether simply to expose another mask cannot be ascertained" (Tanner xxiii). What we are left with is an anarchic welter of autonomous agencies, amid a eunomic dissolution that ominously posits the interior blankness of the American "no-man."

Poe and Melville scrutinize the (self-)destructive potential lurking in autonomy—an *auto-nomia* spreading ulcerously in private selves, poised to blaze through the nomistic (and natural) world like fire. Emerson,

Thoreau, and Whitman's deified selves are accompanied here by a diminishment of both the benignancy and potency of *themis*. *Enthusiasmos* begets a finally self-predatory, self-consumptive autonomy, in anticipation of the increasingly baleful self-law represented in the work of Hemingway, Mailer, and McCarthy, as well as the self-canceling hyperautonomy of DeLillo and Shteyngart.

5 /   Isolates and Outlaws

As social conditions become more equal, the number of persons increases who, although they are neither rich enough nor powerful enough to exercise any great influence over their fellow-creatures, have nevertheless acquired or retained sufficient education and fortune to satisfy their own wants. They owe nothing to any man, they expect nothing from any man; they acquire the habit of always considering themselves as standing alone, and they are apt to imagine that their whole destiny is in their own hands. Thus not only does democracy make every man forget his ancestors, but it hides his descendants, and separates his contemporaries from him; it throws him back forever upon himself alone, and threatens in the end to confine him entirely within the solitude of his own heart.

—TOCQUEVILLE, *DEMOCRACY IN AMERICA*

The work of Ernest Hemingway in the 1920s, represented in this chapter by several short stories as well as the novels *The Sun Also Rises* (1926) and *A Farewell to Arms* (1929), assumes the dissolution of American *eunomia*, and the necessity of seeking personal autonomy not as part of some ultimately communal enterprise—even one as conjectural as Emerson, Thoreau, and Whitman had posited—but in cool detachment from the nomistic world. Where Poe and Melville charted, as it were, the early, explosive, and still rather speculative repercussions of eunomic dissolution, Hemingway anatomizes the givens of its post-traumatic wreckage. The inefficacy of shared rituals, the inadequacy of a general trust in human and divine goodness, and the difficulty of finding a way to (an often elusive and enigmatic) *themis* on one's own terms, are taken for granted. Hemingway's isolates confront an existential void, and in response cultivate a rugged Epicureanism, in the profound ancient sense: within a strictly circumscribed privacy they are fixed in profound skepticism of public ideals (and add to their nomistic withdrawal a strong overlay of Stoic resolve, or so-called "grace under pressure"), and treat sensuous experience as inherently valuable (amounting, in fact, to a kind of devotional connoisseurship of physicality).

Mailer's representation of personal autonomy similarly treats eunomic dissolution as a given, and parallels Hemingway in lauding the masculinist vigor associated with the mythic frontiersman. However, rather than favoring a retreat from one's *nomos* and the protection of a limited self-pasture, he celebrates the positive, creative potential of the self's private communion with *themis*. Departing from Hemingway in resurrecting the Transcendentalists' faith in the gigantic powers of the deified self, Mailer in fact grants the autonomous person the power to challenge, and model the revitalization of, the disesteemed nomistic world. He thus conceives of the possible restoration of (a rather lurid) American *eunomia*. Nevertheless, his outlaws—tracked here in selected works, from *The Naked and the Dead* (1948) through *The Executioner's Song* (1979)—underscore, with increasing pessimism, how vainly predatory and destructive a rugged personal autonomy is likely to be in the last half of the twentieth century. Such figures pursue a neo-Transcendentalist version of the frontiersman's sacred hunt within urban spaces, and they erupt, very often, into open conflict with nomistic authorities. As the Mailer of the late 1970s would concede, his own "antidote" to the sickly American *nomos* seems inevitably implicated in *un*regenerative violence and nagging psychopathologies. In it we find prefigurations of the universal rapacity of McCarthy's Judge, along with the contemporary negations and centripetal sterility of DeLillo and Shteyngart's hyperautonomists.

Mark Twain's *Adventures of Huckleberry Finn* (1884) concludes with its restless narrator conjuring a frontier life beyond the reach of a disesteemed (and frequently violent) "sivilisation," the *nomos* from which, it seems, he must detach himself in order to claim his autonomy:

> Tom's most well, now, and got his bullet around his neck on a watch-guard for a watch, and is always seeing what time it is, and so there ain't nothing more to write about, and I am rotten glad of it, because if I'd a knowed what a trouble it was to make a book I wouldn't a tackled it and ain't agoing to no more. But I reckon I got to light out for the Territory ahead of the rest, because Aunt Sally she's going to adopt me and sivilize me and I can't stand it. I been there before. (Twain 354)

Before "the rest" can catch up, Huck will seek communion with Nature in what remains of the American arcadia—on more gentle terms, perhaps, than those of Boone and Bumppo, but with a similar commitment to solitude. As Leo Marx reminds us, however, Twain knew that similar opportunities for nomistic escape were, in his own day, plainly running out: "By 1884, to be sure, the idea of a refuge in the 'Territory' was almost as tenuous as the idea of floating downstream on a raft. Six years later the Superintendent of the Census declared that the frontier no longer existed" (Marx 340).

Hemingway famously claimed that "All modern American literature comes from one book, [*Huckleberry Finn*]" (Hemingway, *Green* 23), and though he likely meant to cite the influence, above all, of Twain's construction of plain American speech, it is Huck's alienated and imperiled self-pasture that sets the definitive literary terms of his own work. How to live in a territory claimed by discredited and often inimical authorities is the challenge faced by Hemingway's protagonists, who tend to be nomadic (from *nomos* as "pasture") in body and spirit. Usually, they possess something akin to Odysseus's polytropic skills—a keen if cynical knowledge of nomistic codes, and an ability to adapt to environments presenting both physical and psychic threats—but unlike their ancient predecessor have no ultimate home other than what they can fashion, as they wander, for themselves. These figures resemble belated frontiersmen, with little actual wilderness, and almost nothing of the themistic potency of the sacred hunt, left to them. Their survival is played out upon the existentialist's empty ground, their autonomy radical, isolating, (self-)contingent.

Robert Penn Warren's seminal assessment of Hemingway's work aptly suggests the terms, and some of the lineage, of that ground. Linking Hemingway with a series of nineteenth-century American and British authors, he sees him as dramatizing the culmination of several decades of intellectual and spiritual demoralization: "[Hemingway's] is the world of, to use Bertrand Russell's phrase, 'secular hurryings through space.' It is the God-abandoned world, the world of Nature-as-all . . . the world with nothing at center" (Warren 42). *Themis* is reduced in this reckoning to something like Callicles's notion of a blind, insentient force, leveling all in pitiless competition for survival. But where Melville's Ahab sees in that force an "outrageous strength, with an inscrutable malice sinewing it" (*Moby Dick* 178), and is catalyzed into titanic self-assertion, Hemingway's Epicureans know the existential void as a familiar thing, not to be challenged with imperial willpower but survived, somehow, in private retreat. Hemingway's Frederic Henry provides a bitter summary of its brutality, and implies the futility of any grand resistance to it, in *A Farewell to Arms*: "If people bring so much courage to this world the world has to kill them to break them, so of course it kills them. The world breaks every one and afterward many are strong at the broken places. But those that will not break it kills. It kills the very good and the very gentle and the very brave impartially. If you are none of these you can be sure it will kill you too but there will be no special hurry" (*Farewell* 249). What Poe explored as the pathologies of privacy, the shadows of the inward journey for the nomistically detached, are known to the isolates of Hemingway's world, too. Their struggle for autonomy will involve finding a suitable place for their retreat, for subduing (but always grimly conceding the ascendance of) what Melville dubbed "inscrutable malice."

Hemingway's skepticism of the Transcendentalist legacy and its ostensible naivety about the problem of evil finds an illuminating prologue in Melville's own annotations of Emerson's essays. As William Braswell notes, the following remark, scribbled into the margin of "The Poet," "sums up very well Melville's criticism of Emerson" (Braswell 331): "His gross and astonishing errors & illusions spring from a self-conceit so intensely intellectual and calm that at first one hesitates to call it by its right name" (qtd. in Braswell 331). Emerson confidently asserts in this essay the potential of "the poet"—as representative of any autonomous person—to interpret experience afresh and achieve a mastering knowledge under the tutelage of Nature's God: "As the eyes of Lyncaeus were said to see through the earth, so the poet turns the world to glass, and shows us all things in their right series and procession. For through that better perception he stands one step nearer to things, and sees the flowing or metamorphosis. . . . He knows why the plain or meadow of space was strown with these flowers we call suns, and moons and stars; why the great deep is adorned with animals, with men, and gods; for in every word he speaks he rides on them as the horses of thought" (Emerson, "Poet" 296). Underlining "He knows," Melville sardonically undercuts Emerson's optimism with another annotation: "Would some poet be pleased to tell us 'why.' Will Mr. E.?" (Braswell 324).

Melville's skepticism is elaborated in Hemingway's isolates, whose interpretations of their experiences are characteristically circumspect and provisional. It is not for them to master the world, but to find a corner within it that can, if only tentatively, be made orderly and hospitable. They seek, that is, a "clean well-lighted place," like the suicidal "old man" and the insomniac waiter who serves him in one of Hemingway's most famous stories. Here, a paltry and vulnerable self confronts the encroaching darkness and what is feared to be a threatening themistic void: "It was all a nothing and a man was nothing too. It was only that and light was all it needed and a certain cleanness and order. Some lived in it and never felt it but he knew it all was *nada y pues nada y nada y pues nada*. Our *nada* who art in *nada*, *nada* be thy name thy kingdom *nada* thy will be *nada* in *nada* as it is in *nada*" (291).

Private, precarious sanctuaries set against a backdrop of annihilation are, indeed, the typical tableaux of Hemingway's world. In "Indian Camp," Nick Adams, as a young and up to this point (apparently) sheltered boy, witnesses his father perform a crude, anesthetic-free caesarian section on an Indian woman, before discovering that the woman's husband has slit his own throat because he could not bear the sounds of her agony. "'But her screams are not important,'" Nick's father had lectured his son, "I don't hear them because they are not important" ("Indian" 68). In stunned revolt from this icy pragmatism and its gory results, Nick heads home feeling "quite sure that he would never die" (70), a conviction that will not last into adulthood. One of the "interludes" from *In Our Time*, which finds Nick shot in the spine and slumped against a wall in Italy during the war, starkly defines the vulnerability of this new frontiersman:

> *Two Austrian dead lay in the rubble in the shade of the house. Up the street were other dead. Things were getting forward in the town. It was going well. Stretcher bearers would be along any time now. Nick turned his head carefully and looked at Rinaldi. "Senta Rinaldi. Senta. You and me we've made a separate peace." Rinaldi lay still in the sun breathing with difficulty. "Not patriots." Nick turned his head carefully away smiling sweatily. Rinaldi was a disappointing audience.* ("Chapter VI" 105)

Unlike Bumppo in *Deerslayer*, who wakes into a vital and empowering sense of Nature's God after killing an Indian, Nick's war experience leaves him an isolated, belated, ironic "American Adam," skeptical of his fatherland and its ideals. His experiences in "The Battler"—suckerpunched off a train, then threatened by a deranged man as he seeks sanctuary at a campfire in the woods—set the hazardous terms of his alienated postwar life. Unlike Ahab, who will hunt, until his own extinction, "All that most maddens and torments; all that stirs up the lees of things; all truth with malice in it; all that cracks the sinews and cakes the brain; all the subtle demonisms of life and thought; all evil . . . visibly personified, and made practically assailable in Moby-Dick" (*Moby Dick* 200), Nick must content himself with the prospect of throwing a stone, some day, at "[that] lousy crut of a brakeman" ("Battler" 97) who assaulted him.

In "Big Two-Hearted River," we discover Nick alone on a fishing trip, his separation from any community decidedly unpeaceful. He will seek autonomy in private, beyond an abandoned nomistic world figured here as "burned-over country" ("Big" 163). Whereas Bumppo's wilderness immersion deepens his sense of the laws of Nature that govern human communities, Nick recognizes no communal bonds, and no ordering authority other than that which he can project out of himself. Eunomic dissolution is confirmed in his rendering of other humans as contaminating presences within the natural world: "If a trout was touched with a dry hand, a white fungus attacked the unprotected spot. Years before when he had fished crowded streams, with fly fisherman ahead of him and behind him, Nick had again and again come on dead trout, furry with white fungus, drifted against a rock, or floating belly up in some pool. Nick did not like to fish with other men on the river. Unless they were of your party, they spoiled it" (176).

In his flight from "other men," Nick struggles with internal (and enigmatic) agonies unknown to the mythic frontiersman. Survival means, in part, mastering the hostile elements of his own mind: "Nick felt happy [because] he had left everything behind, the need for thinking, the need to write, other needs. It was all back of him" (164). Violence and death are now managed, not merely physically, but as symbolic forms, displaced so as to confer a sense of mastery: "Nick took [the grasshopper] by the head and held him while he threaded the slim hook under his chin, down through his thorax and into the last segments of his abdomen. The grasshopper took hold of the hook with his front feet, spitting tobacco juice on it. Nick dropped him into the water" (175). In his desire for *ataraxia* (tranquility) and *aponia* (absence of pain), as well as in his efforts to "live unobtrusively" (*lathe biosas*), Nick in fact recalls, albeit with a strong suggestion of personal pathology, the ancient Epicureans. Self-pasture is resolutely, even desperately private here, structured (and buttressed) by idiosyncratic rituals meant to secure reliable pleasure and avoid crippling pain:

Across the open mouth of the tent Nick fixed cheesecloth to keep out mosquitoes. He crawled inside under the mosquito bar with various things from the pack to put at the head of the bed under the slant of the canvas. Inside the tent the light came through the brown canvas. It smelled pleasantly of canvas. Already there was something mysterious and homelike. Nick was happy as he crawled inside the tent. He had not been unhappy all day. This was different though. Now things were done. There had been this to do. Now it was done. It had been a hard trip. He was very tired. That was done. He had made his camp. He was settled. Nothing could touch him. It was a good place to camp. He was there, in the good place. He was in his home where he had made it. Now he was hungry. (167)

In this "good place" (or private utopia: Greek *eu* "good" + *topos* "place"), Nick cultivates a redemptive self-law separate from his ruined *nomos*. An Epicurean in the modern sense, too, he relies on refined sensuous experience, organized on his own terms, as the reliable "ground" of value in his privacy:

> Across the river in the swamp, in the almost dark, he saw a mist rising. He looked at the tent once more. All right. He took a full spoonful from the plate.
> "Chrise," Nick said. "Geezus Chrise," he said happily. (168)

A (reduced, tenuous) themistic power becomes available here in Nick's ritualized behavior and the pleasure it provides. Looming over that communion, however, is the presence of the "swamp," an image of what Poe explored as the self's dark places, where one is liable to drown in one's privacy: "Nick did not want to go in there now. He felt a reaction against deep wading with the water deepening up under his armpits, to hook big trout in places impossible to land them. In the swamp the banks were bare, the big cedars came together overhead, the sun did not come through, except in patches; in the fast deep water, in the half light, the fishing would be tragic. In the swamp fishing was a tragic adventure. Nick did not want it. He did not want to go down the stream any farther to-day" (180).

Knowing how to reap and regulate pleasure becomes of paramount importance for Hemingway's isolates, not just as a means of surviving the swampy depths of one's own privacy, but in dealing, at whatever level of detachment, with the nomistic world. Jake Barnes from *The Sun Also Rises*, who has been wounded in a manner similar to Ahab, pursues a characteristically modest strategy of adaptation: "Enjoying living was learning to get your money's worth and knowing when you had it. . . . Perhaps as you went along you did learn something. I did not care what it was all about. All I wanted to know was how to live in it" (148).

Eating and drinking, appreciating the aesthetic and moral value of the bullfight, managing one's own emotions, take on, for Jake, a themistic authority. His relation to that authority can often seem trivial, however, for his Epicureanism has nothing of Jefferson's profound engagement with the examined life. Thinking too much, especially about abstract matters, is yet another source of pain, and sensuous indulgence carries with it, always, a quality of desperation. A spiritual blight is widespread here—

> "What's the matter? You sick?"
> "Yes."
> "Everybody's sick. I'm sick, too." (*Sun* 16)

—and communal rituals often seem like simulacra of the authentic experiences one has in private: "It was like certain dinners I remember from the war. There was much wine, an ignored tension, and a feeling of things coming that you could not prevent happening. Under the wine I lost the disgusted feeling and was happy. It seemed they were all such nice people" (146).

In "Prudence," Emerson—who never went to battle or sailed the high seas himself—emphasizes the kind of courage made possible by personal autonomy (in the sense of the Greek *nemo* as "to have to oneself or possess"):

> Entire self-possession may make a battle very little more danger-
> ous to life than a match at foils or at football. Examples are cited
> by soldiers of men who have seen the cannon pointed and the fire
> given to it, and who have stepped aside from the path of the ball.
> The terrors of the storm are chiefly confined to the parlor and the
> cabin. The drover, the sailor, buffets it all day, and his health renews
> itself at as vigorous a pulse under the sleet as under the sun of June.
> ("Prudence" 223)

Melville—who knew the high seas all too well—added an ironic annotation to this passage: "'To one who has weathered Cape Horne as a common sailor what stuff all this is'" (qtd. in Braswell 329). Optimism, he implies, is born of naïve abstraction; practical experience dissolves it. It is just such experience that propels Frederic Henry's skepticism of shared ideals: "I was always embarrassed by the words sacred, glorious, and sacrifice and the expression in vain" (*Farewell* 184–85). After being condemned by the nomistic world, he rejects his communal ties in search of another "separate peace" (and in doing so he conspicuously lacks, of course, Antigone's vigorous themistic commitments, and Socrates's unflinching loyalty to state authorities even after they unjustly sentence him to death):

> You saw emptily, lying on your stomach, having been present
> when one army moved back and another came forward. You had
> lost your cars and your men as a floorwalker loses the stock of his
> department in a fire. There was, however, no insurance. You were
> out of it now. You had no more obligation. . . . I was not against
> them. I was through. I wished them all the luck. There were the
> good ones, and the brave ones, and the calm ones and the sensible
> ones, and they deserved it. But it was not my show any more and I
> wished this bloody train would get to Mestre and I would eat and
> stop thinking. I would have to stop. (*Farewell* 232)

To be "out of it" is to risk the terrors of solitude, and a critical test of Frederic's autonomy, similarly faced by Nick and Jake, involves managing his private thoughts. Turning away from a broader community, Frederic turns *to* physical realities: "Abstract words such as glory, honor, courage, or hallow were obscene beside the concrete names of villages, the numbers of roads, the names of rivers, the numbers of regiments and the dates" (185). His search for reliable pleasures has its own odor of inconsequence, however, and suggests a merely negative value (an escape *from* unnavigable realities): "I was not made to think. I was made to eat. My God, yes. Eat and drink and sleep with Catherine" (233).

Violence is an integral part of Hemingway's world, since it is against the palpable threat of an utter loss of autonomy (in death) that his protagonists construct their rituals. The bulwarks around one's self-pasture hold back the threat of ultimate self-annihilation. Encounters with violence, as Mailer's outlaw heroes will contend, thus become revelatory of *themis*, though in a manner that, once again, suggests a trivial reduction of the sacred hunt:

> [The bull] charged straight for the steers and two men ran out
> from behind the planks and shouted, to turn him. He did not
> change his direction and the men shouted: "Hah! Hah! Toro!" and
> waved their arms; the two steers turned sideways to take the shock,
> and the bull drove into one of the steers.
> "Don't look," I said to Brett. She was watching, fascinated.
> "Fine," I said. "If it doesn't buck you."

"I saw it," she said. "I saw him shift from his left to his right horn."

"Damn good!" (*Sun* 140)

Bullfighting itself represents for Hemingway a model of the self's efforts to confront and master death. The bullfighter Pedro Romero epitomizes such mastery as he achieves his moment of *aristeia* in the bullring: "He killed not as he had been forced to by the last bull, but as he wanted to" (22). The *communal* dimension of Romero's action (which clearly belongs to an archaic *nomos* quite alien to that of the novel's American ex-pats) is decidedly unavailable to Jake, but its elements of courage and self-discipline model for him the heroic possibilities of autonomy available, if only vestigially and on tightly circumscribed, private terms, in the contemporary era. Frederic Henry demonstrates his own capacity for violence in dispatching a deserter under his command:

> I opened up my holster, took the pistol, aimed at the one who had talked the most, and fired. I missed and they both started to run. I shot three times and dropped one. The other went through the hedge and was out of sight. I fired at him through the hedge as he ran across the field. The pistol clicked empty and I put in another clip. I saw it was too far to shoot at the second sergeant. He was far across the field, running, his head held low. I commenced to reload the empty clip. (204)

Though undertaken within the legal compass of his duties, the coolness of the action suggests the frontiersman's (or cowboy's) ease with violence, but also helps confirm Frederic's sense of disgust with those duties, and desire for his own nomistic desertion.

As Poe insisted, the journey inward reveals myriad pathologies: an untamed menace lurks in the void, and any "separate peace" achieved through private rituals is always threatened by renewed hostilities. What haunts and confines Hemingway's characters is an awareness of the emptiness behind all private ritual, the impossibility of accessing, or projecting from oneself, any stable, adequate themistic order. Wherever they go, they bring an apprehension of the existential void, and its attendant volatilities, with them. After Mailer's recuperative efforts—a positive, if febrile, rendering of the existentialist's construction of something out of *nada*—we will encounter in McCarthy's *Blood Meridian* the destructive climax of American autonomy, and the desolation of any physical or social ground on which that autonomy might be claimed.

From his early renown upon the publication of his debut novel, *The Naked and the Dead* (1948), Norman Mailer was keenly interested in his status as a public intellectual and the influence he might have not just in interpreting contemporary American culture, but in shaping it. His most notorious announcement of his ambitions—which parallels Whitman's efforts to celebrate himself and augment a version of *celebritas*—came in 1959, near the beginning of a collection of self-conscious self-promotion titled *Advertisements for Myself*: *"The sour truth is that I am imprisoned with a perception which will settle for nothing less than making a revolution in the consciousness of our time"* (Mailer, *Advertisements* 15; italics in original). For Mailer at this stage of his career, the revolution he envisioned, and hoped to illustrate in his writing, held the promise of revitalizing American autonomy.

Mailer follows Whitman not just in his pursuit of celebrity—with its attendant assumptions about a deified self in charge of its own making—but in his emphasis on the divinity of the body and interest in the self's growth within an *urbs naturae*. Where he is most like Emerson and Thoreau is in the complaint he launches against the contemporary American *nomos*: a "conformist" majority withers the potential of self-law, Mailer claims, enforcing submission to an effete, constricting set of social demands and self-limitations. The "integrity of one's own mind" is, he insists, continually and profoundly under attack from *without*. Mailer followed the Transcendentalists, too, in counseling nomistic detachment and the cultivation of a self invigorated by (or in his terminology, which emphasizes the force of obligation, "imprisoned with") a themistic potency from which the majority have been estranged. In both his essays and his fiction, Mailer was an advocate, moreover, of a personal (and often incendiary) *daemon*, one which exhorted the self to expressions of primitivist vigor. It is this last quality that Mailer admired most in Hemingway, who gave him (in his writing as well as his life) a model for masculinist heroics. But Mailer departs from Hemingway's largely anti-intellectual and apolitical stance by adopting the role of a kind of prescriptive, Romantic mythographer; as such, he complicates the ultimately benign cosmology of his Transcendentalist precursors with an acute concern for the persistence and efficacy of evil. The aggressively antisocial potential lurking in Hemingway's Nick Adams, Jake Barnes, and Frederic Henry, is, however, actualized in Mailer's outlaw heroes, who mix inward journeying and universal self-containment with the mythic frontiersman's active expression of predatory aggression, and often challenge communal authorities directly and violently. In such figures, Mailer reproduces not only the ominous blankness, rootlessness, and polytropic skills of Odysseus, but also the themistic fanaticism—an utter commitment to "higher laws," obviating any routine concerns for self-preservation—of Antigone and Socrates. Mailer's outlaws darken and reduce these imaginative kin, however, and come to seem, in the limited contemporary space of their self-pasture and its eunomic dissolution, like (destructive) martyrs for a barren cause. Mailer's revolutionary ambition thus represents a troubled late stage in the growth of American autonomy, for he shows us both the enduring allure of self-pasture—an attempt to limn its most positive, creative potential—*and* the increasing complications and pathologies of its expression in his own historical period.

Mailer's *The Naked and the Dead* explores the experiences of a group of soldiers fighting in the South Pacific during World War II. The novel introduces two characters—General Cummings, a fascist apologist, and Sergeant Croft, a brutal leader bent on imposing his will at whatever cost—who begin an incendiary procession of outlaws in Mailer's work: among them, Marion Faye in *The Deer Park* (1955), the "hipster" in the essay "The White Negro," Stephen Rojack and Barney Oswald Kelly in *An American Dream*, Gary Gilmore in *The Executioner's Song*, Dix Butler in *Harlot's Ghost* (1991), and Lee Harvey Oswald in *Oswald's Tale: An American Mystery* (1995). Though Cummings and Croft are ostensibly the novel's villains, Mailer finds something of value in those who, like the more aggressive versions of the mythic frontiersman, are willing and even eager to employ force. Dubbed "The Hunter," Croft is marked out by an affinity for cold, unintellectualized predation: "*he was efficient and strong and usually empty and his main cast of mind was a superior contempt toward nearly all other men. He hated weakness and he loved practically nothing. There was a crude unformed vision in his soul and he was rarely conscious of it*" (Mailer, *Naked* 136). Croft's "vision" grants him access to the divine, which he worships through acts of violence. Cummings theorizes such acts in terms redolent of Callicles's "law of nature," invoking an ad-justment of all in bloody competition similar to that articulated by McCarthy's Judge: "[The] only morality of the future is a power morality, and a man who cannot find his adjustment to it is doomed. There's one thing about power. It can flow only from the top down. When there are little surges of resistance at the middle levels, it merely calls for more power to be directed downward, to burn it out" (282).

Cummings and Croft are repellent in their sadistic powermongering, but Mailer lauds their willingness to act and their understanding that violent conflict has a kind of metaphysical primacy and themistic authority, if only in denuded form as brute *physis*. The implication in such characterizations, as Kathryn Hume remarks, is that "a capacity for violence can bring one close to revelation" (Hume 129). In later works, Mailer will parse the qualities of this experience more finely while elaborating his definition of themistic authority, but he suggests its basic terms here in his descriptions of the vivifying awareness one gains through combat of the interconnection of death and life. Intimacy with the facts of predation and death has, according to Mailer, been systematically eradicated in postwar America, but the man who could survive, and indeed flourish, with such intimacy would approximate the "natural" status of the mythic frontiersman, moving comfortably in both the "savage" and the "civilized" worlds. Deprived of any vital imaginative connection to such figures, American selfhood has been stunted and sickened.

It is, for Mailer, nomistic "totalitarianism" that inhibits the contemporary American self, and Cummings prophesies its rise in the nation: "For the past century the entire historical process has been working toward greater and greater consolidation of power. Physical power for this century, an extension of our universe, and a political power, a political organization to make it possible" (281). In the early 1960s, Mailer would closely analyze the "plague" of this kind of organization in a number of essays, collected as *The Presidential Papers* (1964). As he summarizes the concept: "The essence of totalitarianism is that it beheads. It beheads individuality, variety, dissent, extreme possibility, romantic faith, it blinds vision, deadens instinct, it obliterates the past" ("Ninth," *Presidential* 184). The sophistication of sociopolitical control—a rationalization and technologizing of everyday life that banishes awareness of divine influences and converts the potentially autonomous person into "mass man"—amounts to totalitarianism even in a supposed liberal democracy. In "Superman Comes to the Supermarket" (1961), an essay about the 1960 Democratic Convention, Mailer describes how what he sees as America's seminal and sustaining myth, that the country provides opportunities to participate in heroism and become a hero oneself, has endured in spite of the rise of a technocratic, rationalized age:

> And this myth, that each of us was born to be free, to wander, to have adventure and to grow on the waves of the violent, the perfumed, and the unexpected, had a force which could not be tamed

no matter how the nation's regulators—politicians, ideologues, psychoanalysts, builders, executives and endless communicators—would brick-in the modern life with hygiene upon sanity, and middle-brow homily over platitude; the myth would not die. . . . [I]t was as if the message locked within the labyrinth of the genes would insist that violence was locked with creativity, and adventure was the secret of love. ("Superman," *Presidential* 39–40)

Mailer writes of this wide-ranging phenomenon, again in the "Superman" essay: "the incredible dullness wreaked upon the American landscape in Eisenhower's eight years has been the triumph of the corporation. A tasteless, sexless, odorless sanctity in architecture, manners, modes, styles has been the result. Eisenhower embodied half the needs of the nation, the needs of the timid, the petrified, the sanctimonious, and the sluggish" (43). It is, says Mailer, "*death [that] the Twentieth Century is seeking to avoid*" (176). The death-seeker was Mailer's antidote—an urban frontiersman, alive to adventure and risk, eager to participate in whatever might be left of the sacred hunt.

Writing in 1948, Robert Warshow could point to the gangster of popular films as the genuine modern seer, sadly at home in the microcosmic metropolis:

The gangster is the man of the city, with the city's language and knowledge, with its queer and dishonest skills and terrible daring, carrying his life in his hands like a placard, like a club. For everyone else, there is at least the theoretical possibility of another world—in that happier American culture which the gangster denies, the city does not really exist; it is only a more crowded and more brightly lit country—but for the gangster there is only the city; he must inhabit it in order to personify it: not the real city, but that dangerous and sad city of the imagination which is so much more important, which is the modern world. And the gangster—though there are real gangsters—is also, and primarily, a creature of the imagination. The real city, one might say, produces only criminals; the imaginary city produces the gangster: he is what we want to be and what we are afraid we may become. (Warshow 131)

That figure's "unlimited possibility of aggression" (132) was his deepest attraction and deepest liability: detached from *nomos* and the lives comfortably sustained there, he would individuate himself in an orgasm of self-liberation, then ensure his final, isolated annihilation by nomistic avengers. Wayne J. Douglass, in his reflection on Warshow's essay, rightly calls the "psychopath" the gangster's "logical successor," a figure who rebels against the depersonalizing bureaucracies and repressive imperatives of postwar America, and "for whom the emotional euphoria accompanying the commission of violent crimes was more important than material gain" (Douglass 30). Here the moment of *aristeia*, in which the Homeric warrior had realized his human potential in battle while securing gains for his fellow warriors, uneasily combines the themistic derangement explored in Poe and Melville, which blazingly consumes the self, with the *positive* self-possession and self-inhabitance affirmed by Emerson and Thoreau in their enthusiastic triumphs over the inhibiting nomistic world.

In "The White Negro," Mailer conjures his own "creature of the imagination," resembling Warshow's polytropic gangster in his dangerous but enviable rebellion, and Douglass's psychopath in his free emotional expression. This figure promises liberation from the nomistic tyranny of postwar America, which Mailer characterizes while striking a familiar Emersonian chord: conformity to social codes threatens the self's creativity and access to "natural," themistically sanctioned energies. What Emerson says of the anomic bent of virtue—"a man or a company of men, plastic and permeable to principles, by the law of nature must overpower and ride all cities, nations, kings, rich men, poets, who are not" ("Self-Reliance" 159)—Mailer echoes, explicitly endorsing the expression of aggressively physical actions, while also demonstrating a greater tolerance for, and interest in imagining the ambiguous endowments of, so-called "Devil's children." Though acting on his own and for himself, the "white negro"—equivalent to the "white savage" of frontier mythology—foretells for Mailer a widespread rebellion and reclamation of autonomy in the "conformist" and consumerist cities he has inherited and imaginatively commands. He is Whitman with a gun and a grudge, a contemporary polytropic self, an American Odysseus, who has "[seen] the cities, and [known] the minds, of many men" (*Odyssey* 1.1, 3). Devoted to a *themis* accessed privately and at odds with the nomistic world, he is also a dark affiliate of Antigone and Socrates.

Mailer begins his consideration of the psychopathic type by identifying the spiritual consequences of fascism, speculating on "the psychic havoc of the concentration camps and the atom bomb" for postwar Americans ("White Negro" 311). Personal autonomy, he claims, has been radically threatened in these "years of conformity and depression," and the nation, losing control of death to enormous technocratic forces, has also lost contact with a definitive source of vitality. Mailer places his hope, against dismal cultural circumstances, in his identification of (and with) a newly emerging kind of man, "the American existentialist—the hipster" (312). This figure responds to the restrictions of contemporary life by "[encouraging] the psychopath" in himself, rejecting nomistic conventions, particularly those relating to sex and violence, which would inhibit him. Mailer explicitly nods to Thoreau in diagnosing social conformity and prescribing a cure: "The unstated essence of Hip, its psychopathic brilliance, quivers with the knowledge that new kinds of victories increase one's power for new kinds of perception; and defeats, the wrong kind of defeats, attack the body and imprison one's energy until one is jailed in the prison air of other people's habits, other people's defeats, boredom, *quiet desperation*, and muted icy self-destroying rage" (312–13; italics added).

Mailer endorses here a turn backward to the mythic frontiersman and his imagined qualities of rugged autonomy, sensual indulgence, and physical adventure, but now—following Whitman—within the "Nature" to be found in the crowded urban wilds. The choice confronting Americans is sharply defined: "One is Hip or one is Square (the alternative which each new generation coming into American life is beginning to feel), one is a rebel or one conforms, one is a frontiersman in the Wild West of American night life, or else a Square cell, trapped in the totalitarian tissues of American society, doomed willy-nilly to conform if one is to succeed" (312–13). Mailer's philosophy of "Hip" does not shy from violent excesses, for it promises to "return us to ourselves" by "envisag[ing] acts of violence as the catharsis which prepares growth" (328). This means a "return" not just to something like Boone's and Bumppo's primitivist dynamism, but to infancy and the pleasure principle. The psychopath, Mailer asserts, is an intriguing model of a kind of prenomistic being, perfectly at home within a Calliclean ad-justment of naturalized antagonists. His "fundamental decision," like that of McCarthy's Judge, is "to try to live the infantile fantasy" and "go back to the source of [his] creation" (319). What might look like acts of extreme and wholly pernicious deviance—mere antisocial indulgence, unredeemed and contemptible—are reshaped by this logic into examples of a vigorous autonomy no longer possible for "mass man."

If his cultural and geographic origins are to be found somewhere in frontier America, and his psychological wellspring in the id, the hipster's racial locus is the black man (as Cooper's was the "savage" Indian). The "Negro," suggests Mailer in what is meant to be a compliment, is a model toward which many white conformists might aspire, for blacks have been existentially energized by continually having to confront mortal challenges in racist America. And in fact, claims Mailer, in the 1950s many whites were indeed beginning to carry out this sort of racial modeling and invigoration, "[drifting] out at night looking for action with a black man's code to fit their facts" (315). Liberated from conventional repression, the hipster achieves a special closeness to the unconscious, which comes to stand for "Nature's God" (here not Calliclean at all, but in fact robust and sentient in its engagement with human agents, as Emerson, Thoreau, and Whitman had insisted):

> But to be with it is to have grace, is to be closer to the secrets of that inner unconscious life which will nourish you if you can hear it, for you are then nearer to that God which every hipster believes is located in the senses of the body, that trapped, mutilated and nonetheless megalomaniacal God who is It, who is energy, life, sex, force, the Yoga's *prana*, the Reichian's orgone, Lawrence's "blood," Hemingway's "good," the Shavian life-force; "It"; God; not the God of the churches but the unachievable whisper of mystery within the sex, the paradise of limitless energy and perception just beyond the next wave of the next orgasm. (324–25)

The hipster regresses, and in doing so becomes, like Bumppo at his baptism as "Hawkeye," another American Adam: "standards inherited from the past" (326) are personalized or simply ignored, and "the truth is not what one has felt yesterday or what one expects to feel tomorrow but rather truth is no more nor less than what one feels at each instant in the perpetual climax of the present" (327). Jeffersonian autonomy prudently defined "the sum of good government [. . . as restraining] men from injuring one another," while "[leaving] them otherwise free to regulate their own pursuits of industry and improvement" (Jefferson, "First Inaugural" 494). Mailer would, at his most enthusiastic, risk those injuries, envisioning a radical autonomy that might reverse the withdrawal of Hemingway's isolates and yet escape the whole nomistic world: "the nihilism of Hip proposes as its final tendency that every social restraint and category be removed, and the affirmation implicit in the proposal is that man would then prove to be more creative than murderous and so would not destroy himself" (328).

An American Dream gives us a version of the "white negro" in Stephen Rojack, the novel's narrator and protagonist. Rojack is a war hero who has built a successful career first as a politician and then as a popular psychologist, but he is deeply unhappy with his conventional life and haunted by memories of combat. Most immediate among his oppressors is his wife, Deborah, whom he considers to be in league with demonic forces. Rojack's definitive act is to rise against these powers by murdering her. His experience of violence and death in the war apparently initiates his conversion to a sort of frontier Transcendentalism: an Emersonian trust in the divinity of the self, combined with an absorption of energies from a racialized Other (the inheritance of Boone and Bumppo) and commitment to themistically sanctioned predation (a concoction that Philip Rahv famously criticized as a "hipster's fantasy," in which "the self becomes so absolutized, so unchecked by reality, as to convert itself with impunity into the sole arbiter of good and evil" [Rahv 2]). After murdering his wife, Rojack confirms his full entry into "Nature," here a supernatural world of ferocious conflict and hyperarousal. Whitmanic urban wandering and erotic disinhibition gain new, darker aspects as, traveling through New York City and "inhaling great draughts of space" (Whitman, "Song of the Open Road" line 58) he comes to rely on "the very intensity of his private vision" (Mailer, "White Negro" 316) and his "inner experience of the possibilities within death" (316). Rojack's mistress notes that after he killed his wife, he looked "painted with a touch of magic" (165). Sex and violence are intimately linked in this realm, while life and death emerge as codependents. The experience recalls the malevolence and nomistic alienation glimpsed by Poe's narrator in "The Man of the Crowd," but here the city is navigated by a heroic urban frontiersman. Battling his wife, and bedding the mistress of a dangerous black man, Rojack claims a risky autonomy, idiosyncratically fulfilling (in ways the sage of Concord would, of course, have found both baffling and horrendous) Emerson's pledge that no law will be sacred to him but that of his own nature.

The divine presences operating within or behind the world's appearances—accessible only to those with the heightened sensitivities Mailer typically attributes to "psychopaths"—are made visible by his "secret frightened romance with the phases of the moon" (15), an "appreciation" (10) gained when as a soldier he killed several men under a beguiling lunar light. What makes Rojack's effort particularly *American*—at least by Mailer's reckoning—is, first, its emphasis on redeeming possibilities for the autonomous person against the threats of a constricting *nomos*, particularly through aggressive encounters with hostile others; and second, the self's assumption of divine powers (which are, as for the Transcendentalists, universally available). What makes it particularly *contemporary* are the hypersophisticated forces—technological, bureaucratic, commercial—marshaled against the aspirant to autonomy. The "totalitarianism" prophesied by General Cummings in *The Naked and the Dead* is in full metastasis here: Rojack is confounded in his efforts to get free of his wife by a sinister network of influence involving the highest levels of American government, the Mafia, the CIA, the media, and big business. To rise against these powers is, according to the author's narrative terms, a heroic act in pursuit of a life-augmenting autonomy.

The ultimate barriers to such pursuit are implied, however, by the conclusion of the novel. Rojack departs declaring he will light out, like Huckleberry Finn, for a territory more mythic than real. Such a protagonist may seek private communion with *themis* in the *urbs naturae*, but any world that might support him, natural or artificial, is at last elusive. Confrontations with death could, Mailer claimed in "The White Negro," bring special, if expensive, knowledge: "There is a depth of desperation to the condition which enables one to remain in life only by engaging death, but the reward is their knowledge that what is happening at each instant of the electric present is good or bad for them, good or bad for their cause, their love, their action, their need" ("White Negro" 316). An increasing inability to find a place to meet those challenges, and the resulting derangement of energies—which take a self-destructive turn—become much more prominent among the desperate rebels of Mailer's later work.

By the late 1970s, the revolution in consciousness Mailer had hoped for had manifestly not arrived, while the state and the corporation continued to augment their sprawling powers. Appearing a little more than two decades after the publication of "The White Negro," *The Executioner's Song*, a partly fictionalized account of the last few months of the life of convicted double-murderer Gary Gilmore, reveals a significant reevaluation of heroic psychopathy and its potential for reclaiming a fertile (if dangerous) self-pasture. The pointless destructiveness of individual violence becomes a major concern here, along with the failure of American spaces—and "the West," with its mythic associations, in particular—as legitimate sites for self-actualization. Mailer's interest in Gilmore's idiosyncratic commitments, and the kernel of invaluable autonomy they ostensibly reveal, competes with his sense of the wastefulness and futility of the outlaw's life.

Gilmore lives in a geographic region that evokes, in its wide and largely barren spaces, the emptiness or exhaustion of the mythic frontiersman's fertile hunting grounds. In his discussion of the spiritual malaise that seems to afflict so many of the characters in Mailer's novel, Joseph Wenke rightly proposes that "the traditional symbolism of the West is inverted [here], suggesting not limitless possibilities and the transcendental freedom of 'the hero in *space*' but the imaginative paralysis that comes when one feels like an outcast whose fate it is to live in the middle of nowhere" (Wenke 202). A character such as Sergeant Croft might test himself against the land in order to achieve his existential "vision," but Gilmore and his fellow Utahans are, for the most part, clueless in their search for meaningful, growth-inducing challenges. And while Stephen Rojack, for instance, fought *for* something—a mysterious but still palpable themistic liberation—Gilmore's struggles, and especially the culmination of his personal frustrations in homicide, veer toward mere nihilism. The rebellion of the psychopath thus threatens to become not an enabling departure from *nomos*—creatively reworking conventional conscience, restraint, conformity—but a sheer, enervating vacancy. The seeming randomness of Gilmore's murders suggests his unfathomability as a psychopath detached from nomistic convention—a quality Mailer admired and valorized in "The White Negro"—but also his emptiness. There is no sacred hunt left to complete, and the spontaneity, freedom from social rules, and absence of inhibitions of the self-lawed person are directed here toward a pointless catharsis.

Mailer is, however, intent on discovering meaning in the crimes, and part of this is achieved by linking their perpetrator with the author's other gifted psychopaths. Gilmore is said to possess—in descriptions that sometimes verge on the comic—a range of exceptional sensitivities and physical capabilities: "[He] owned the best sense of hearing [his cellmate] Gibbs had ever come across. If there was a case of a man with bionic ears, it was Gary Gilmore. . . . Gibbs had noticed that Gilmore would only average two to three hours [of sleep] . . . He didn't seem to need more" (366). The psychiatric report which Mailer excerpts—composed by Robert J. Howell, Ph.D., a straw man whose lack of imagination Mailer would, earlier in his career, have had much more fun setting ablaze—concludes that Gilmore is blessed with high intelligence but given to antisocial tendencies: "In summary, Gary is a 35-year-old Caucasian single male . . . of superior intellect. There is no evidence of organic brain damage. Gary is basically a personality disorder of the psychopathic or antisocial type" (379). Though Mailer largely keeps his own distinctive narrative voice out of this book, the inadequacy of this type-casting for apprehending the specifics of Gilmore's particularity is made clear enough. A more adventurous psychiatrist, Dr. John Woods, is quoted speculating on the mysteries of the psychopathic mind:

> Woods had long suspected the best-kept secret in psychiatric circles was that nobody understood psychopaths, and few had any notion of psychotics. "Look," he would sometimes be tempted to tell a colleague, "the psychotic thinks he's in contact with spirits from other worlds. He believes he is prey to the spirits of the dead. He's in terror. By his understanding, he lives in a field of evil forces.
>
> "The psychopath," Woods would tell them, "inhabits the same place. It is just that he feels stronger. The psychopath sees himself as a potent force in that field of forces. Sometimes he even believes he can go to war against them, and win. So if he really loses, he is close to collapse, and can be as ghost ridden as a psychotic."
>
> For a moment, Woods wondered if that was the way to build a bridge from the psychopathic to the insane. (397–98)

This is very close to Mailer's sense of psychopathy as a committed theism that subordinates nomistic authorities to a private conception of the divine—a quality linking the psychopath, from darker (and distinctively American) depths, to Socrates and Antigone.

Gilmore's murders are deeply repellent for their brutality and waste of innocent life, but Mailer works hard to mitigate this impression by juxtaposing, as he had done in "The White Negro" ("White Negro" 328), the violence of the state with that of the individual. Gilmore, on the run from vastly superior forces, takes on the aura of the underdog:

> SWAT arrived. Special Weapons and Tactical Team. Two teams of five, one after the other. Moving around in dark blue two-piece fatigue uniforms, with black high-laced jump boots, they looked like paratroopers. Except the word POLICE was spelled out in big yellow letters on their shirts. They were certainly carrying heavy stuff—shotguns, .357 Magnums, semiautomatic rifles, tear gas. The night had turned cool after a hot day, but they were sweating plenty. Those armored vests under the fatigues were hot to carry. (*Executioner's Song* 254)

In these moments, Gilmore becomes the symbolic equivalent of the hopelessly overmatched grizzly bear, run down by helicopters, in Mailer's novel *Why Are We in Vietnam?* (1967). There can be no testing of one's potential in this kind of encounter, for either side, since the technology involved makes the outcome predictable. As Gilmore's girlfriend, Nicole, says of his execution (sounding, perhaps, a little too much like Mailer himself): "The real horror was people lining up to blow somebody away with a lack of passion, a methodical, calculated turning of the machinery of the State against the individual. Why come to terms with it?" (773). Gilmore may have been manipulated and malformed by penal institutions for most of his life, his desperate act of release a cruel destruction of innocents, but he can still, Mailer would assert, claim dignity and valor by demanding—in a reduced replaying of Antigone's and Socrates's themistic *aristeia*—his own death. As Sean McCann concludes of the "limited kind of redemption" available to Gilmore and other characters in the work: "despite the force of social expectations and despite the personal weight of accumulated sins and errors, a determined individual might rescue for him or herself some small measure of honor. *The Executioner's Song* is in this sense, as Mailer subsequently and revealingly described it, a story of 'American virtue'" (McCann 294).

"Eastern Voices," the legal and media interests who intervene to represent Gilmore and his story, take over the second half of Mailer's book. The distinctiveness of Gilmore's life bleeds away as he joins a pantheon of the disparately famous. Given a copy of the first *Time* magazine of 1977, Gilmore is fascinated by a photo spread which includes him in a series of images from the past year. Joining President Carter, Betty Ford, Isabelle Peron, Mao Tse-tung, the *Viking 1*, Henry Kissinger, and Nadia Comeneci is "Gary Gilmore in his Maximum Security prison whites" (*Executioner's Song* 789). Rather than standing apart from his *nomos*, Mailer's outlaw—in a prefiguration of hyperautonomy—is smoothly consumed, as his *celebritas* confirms, within its leveling sensibility.

Mailer's heroic outlaw, obedient to a private *themis* which demands sometimes violent self-assertions, becomes in McCarthy a grotesquely destructive antagonist, and in DeLillo an empty figure absorbed into the very systems of nomistic control that Mailer hoped to revolutionize. Versions of the "white negro" and the "psychopath" seem, for these authors, manifestly exhausted in terms of their potential contribution to a "revolution in the consciousness of our time." While still functioning as cultural critics, they herald the worst symptoms of, rather than the cure for, broad nomistic ills.

6 / Self-Pasture's Sublime (and Bloody) Meridian

> *There was scant room for the coward and the weakling in the ranks of the adventurous frontiersmen—the pioneer settlers who first broke up the wild prairie soil, who first hewed their way into the primeval forest, who guided their white-topped wagons across the endless leagues of Indian-haunted desolation, and explored every remote mountain-chain in the restless quest for metal wealth. Behind them came the men who completed the work they had roughly begun: who drove the great railroad systems over plain and desert and mountain pass; who stocked the teeming ranches, and under irrigation saw the bright green of the alfalfa and the yellow of the golden stubble supplant the gray of the sage-brush desert; who have built great populous cities—cities in which every art and science of civilization are carried to its highest point—on tracts which, when the nineteenth century had passed its meridian, were still known only to the grim trappers and hunters and the red lords of the wilderness with whom they waged eternal war.*
>
> —THEODORE ROOSEVELT, *THE STRENUOUS LIFE*

> *[Recent] splatterpunk Westerns, such as Cormac McCarthy's novel Blood Meridian ... make the case that the Western was really about serial killing all along.*
>
> —MARK SELTZER, *SERIAL KILLERS: DEATH AND LIFE IN AMERICA'S WOUND CULTURE*

In Cormac McCarthy's *Blood Meridian: Or The Evening Redness in the West* (1985), we meet in the formidable and frightening Judge Holden the satanic zenith of American autonomy—a figure wandering the desert spaces of the Southwest in the mid-nineteenth century who is, ultimately, representative of autonomy's late-twentieth-century urban pathologies. The Judge's pronouncements, at times suggestive of grandiose bluster but always profoundly resonant, articulate the bloody climax of a broader Western movement toward radical autonomy culminating in the American sublime and its valorization of the self-lawed person. The Judge's bellicose aim—to identify himself with the world, asserting dominion over all living things as "suzerain of the earth" (McCarthy 198)—constitutes a gory reductio ad absurdum not only of the mythic frontiersman's aggression, but of some of Emerson's essential tropes and assumptions, and thus demonstrates the horrific potential latent in the Transcendentalists' deification of personal autonomy. Rather than becoming the vehicle for a vitalized liberal democracy (as Emerson— and, more complexly, Mailer—ultimately hoped), autonomy as the Judge conceives it is associated with an atomizing, aggressive, consumptive agency, a self-pasturing inveterately hostile to all meaningful social ties and catastrophically predatory on both human and natural worlds. Where Melville saw Nature as finally inexhaustible—"Wherefore, for all these things, we account the whale immortal in his species, however perishable in his individuality. . . . In Noah's flood he despised Noah's Ark; and if ever the world is to be again flooded, like the Netherlands, to kill off its rats, then the eternal whale will still survive, and rearing upon the topmost crest of the equatorial flood, spout his frothed defiance to the skies" (Melville 504)—McCarthy posits human autonomy as a threat to the entire natural world. In mortal conflict with every form of life whose self-law cannot be absorbed into his own, the Judge seeks to become a master consumer of all that stands before him, spreading across the land like a burning ulcer, intent to graze alone on vacant land, wholly self-inhabited and self-pastured.

McCarthy also foretells the implosion of the self, explored fully by DeLillo and Shteyngart, that is characteristic of hyperautonomy. After the closing of the American frontier, the pathologies of self-pasture have transitioned, he suggests, from a centrifugal to a centripetal dynamic, from the liberty of the self to range at will to a pasturing of the self *on* the self.

Blood Meridian gives us a viciously and terminally competitive version of personal autonomy—a self-pasture that can abide no other claims to self-law:

> Whatever exists, he said. Whatever in creation exists without my knowledge exists without my consent.
>
> He looked about at the dark forest in which they were bivouacked. He nodded toward the specimens he'd collected. These anonymous creatures, he said, may seem little or nothing in the world. Yet the smallest crumb can devour us. Any smallest thing beneath yon rock out of men's knowing. Only nature can enslave man and only when the existence of each last entity is routed out and made to stand naked before him will he be properly suzerain of the earth. . . .

The judge placed his hands on the ground. He looked at his inquisitor. This is my claim, he said. And yet everywhere upon it are pockets of autonomous life. Autonomous. In order for it to be mine nothing must be permitted to occur upon it save by my dispensation. (McCarthy 198–99)

A "suzerain" is a "feudal overlord," the ruler of a particular region who remains subject to some greater sovereign. McCarthy's Judge Holden takes himself to be a "suzerain of the earth," free of all subjection save to a quasi-Calliclean *physis*, the agonistic law of nature which is all that remains for him of *themis*. Like Antigone, he appeals to, and claims to act on behalf of, themistic authority in defiance of nomistic convention, but in a pitilessly reduced form of that implied by the Greek heroine: "[War] is the truest form of divination. It is the testing of one's will and the will of another within that larger will which because it binds them is therefore forced to select. War is the ultimate game because war is at last a forcing of the unity of existence. War is god" (249). By these lights, war justifies existence in the sense of an ad-justment, a leveling or even-ing of all in bloody competition, an evening "Redness in the West," as Mailer's Cummings had prophesied: "[The] only morality of the future is a power morality, and a man who cannot find his adjustment to it is doomed" (*Naked* 282). No other source of law—divine or political—has any claim on the warrior next to war itself, and the ethical universe he inhabits is therefore radically bare and flat: "This desert upon which so many have been broken is vast and calls for largeness of heart but it is also ultimately empty. It is hard, it is barren. Its very nature is stone" (McCarthy 330).

The novel tracks the Judge's devilish voracity as he, along with a group of marauding scalp hunters known as the Glanton gang, annihilate human populations along the borderlands of Mexico and the United States in the mid-nineteenth century. Its climax comes with the Judge's murder of the narrative's focal protagonist, "the kid" (hereafter without quotation marks), a member of the gang whose sympathetic tendencies slowly and haltingly emerge in opposition to the "taste for mindless violence" (McCarthy 3) that is his birthright. The gang's efforts portend an autonomy of the most radical kind—a separation from the flesh itself, the last nomistic tie to the human order: "the slant black shapes of the mounted men [were] stenciled across the stone with a definition austere and implacable like shapes capable of violating their covenant with the flesh that authored them and continuing autonomous across the naked rock without reference to sun or man or god" (139). The Judge's worship of *physis* would have him rule, at last, a *nomos* coextensive with himself: he will have identified, denuded, and incorporated "whatever in creation" resists him by remaining unknown, exempt from its declared suzerain, autonomous.

The Judge has rightly been seen as both historically representative (kin to the actual freebooting rogues who "settled" the West, though hyperbolized for artistic effect) and mythically suggestive (a sort of demiurge, preternatural in his potency, incarnating a distinctly American version of—to borrow the Nietzschean vocabulary his self-descriptions approximate—the will to power). Gorily revisionist, *Blood Meridian* presents a critique of the material brutality of westward expansion, and of the ostensibly progressive and divinely sanctioned ideologies of Manifest Destiny and rugged autonomy which lay behind it. By this reckoning, the Judge's war on "autonomous life" expresses a tragic paradox of American history: the nation's implication in the demolition of human resistance, particularly the violent removal of native populations from "empty" land, in the name of a historically unprecedented liberty.

In *Nature,* Emerson posits an American self large enough to contain the world, while insisting on the creative as well as the democratic possibilities of such containment: anyone might renovate and augment himself by claiming, via a radical communion with the natural world, all of Nature's infinite possibilities. Myra Jehlen, referring specifically to the famous "transparent eyeball" passage, notes the totalizing implications of this merging of self and world and its licensing of infinite powers: "In short, Emersonian Transcendentalism is the philosophy of the American incarnation, and its fulfillment in an unlimited individualism whereby the self transcends its mortal limits by taking total possession of an actual world" (Jehlen 77). Thinking of oneself as coterminous with the world "endows the American," Jehlen contends, "with transcendent autonomy," and "through his identification with his world each man becomes an autonomous universe in himself" (123).

Blood Meridian is intimately concerned with the implications of autonomy when it is extended into actual (rather than imaginative) worlds not by devotees of the contemplative life such as Emerson himself—who would, of course, have been horrified by the Judge—but by aggressive autonomists bent on material domination. In a well-known essay, Harold Bloom calls *Blood Meridian* "the authentic American apocalyptic novel" (*How to Read* 254), a judgment we can understand better in light of his analysis of national religiosity in *The American Religion* (1992). A preference for radical separateness defines American faith,

Bloom asserts, inaugurating fabulous possibilities for self-expression as well as antisocial volatilities and forbidding voids: "What the American self has found, since about 1800, is its own freedom—from the world, from time, from other selves. But this freedom is a very expensive torso, because of what it is obliged to leave out: society, temporality, the other. What remains, for it, is solitude and the abyss" (*American Religion* 37). We encounter in Emerson's "transparent eyeball" a seminal expression of the American sublime, which, as Bloom defines it in *Poetry and Repression* (1976), differs from English and Continental models by amplifying the expression of autonomy. The American poet suggests his freedom not merely to renew tradition and so find a place for himself within it, but rather to place that tradition itself in an anterior relation and so celebrate a larger victory for the self: "Not merely rebirth, but the even more hyperbolical trope of self-rebegetting, is the starting point of the last Western Sublime, the great sunset of selfhood in the Evening Land" (*Poetry* 244). Bloom sees Emerson as inaugurating this mode for canonical poets extending from "Whitman, Thoreau, Dickinson on through Hart Crane, Stevens, and our contemporaries" (246). These Americans demand not mere participation in literary tradition, but emancipation from it, which is the newcomer's ultimate triumph. Absorbing all rivals so that "the fathering force or representative tends to disappear into the poetic self or son" (246), the American victor is finally able to find himself alone. Bloom says of this strategy in Emerson (and specifically of the "transparent eyeball" passage): "it accomplishes or prepares for a reversal in which the self is forgotten ('I am nothing') and yet through seeing introjects the fathering force of anteriority. By seeing the transparency, the poet of the American Sublime *contains* the father-god, and so augments the poetic self even as he remembers to forget that self" (247–48).

Just after the transparent eyeball passage, Emerson playfully describes the implications of an identification with the natural world: "The greatest delight which the fields and woods minister is the suggestion of an occult relation between man and the vegetable. I am not alone and unacknowledged. They nod to me, and I to them" (Emerson, *Nature* 6). Whatever precise relations might exist between humanity and nature, the encounter suggests a friendly and fertile communion. Personal renovation and expansion are made possible by Nature's infinite resources, which obligingly await human mastery. In the Judge, however, such mastery declares itself in the most brutal terms: the absorption of all ancestors and rivals, the achievement of an ultimate solitude, the movement into some "great sunset of selfhood in the Evening Land." Though Bloom's essay on the novel places its emphasis elsewhere, his definition of the American sub-lime as involving boundless absorption and "self-rebegetting" (*Poetry* 244) often seems to be satanically satirized in the Judge, with mere imag-inative absorption extended into material reality so that actual things are made to disappear. "[Placing] his hands on the ground" (McCarthy 199), the Judge darkens Emerson's benign claim of "all nature for his dowry and estate" (Emerson, *Nature* 11), his ambition involving not just mastery of the pasturage under his dominion, but a consumptive annihilation. Bloom notes that the Judge "seems to judge the entire earth," and that his "[full] name [Judge Holden] suggests a holding, presumably of sway over all he encounters" (*How to Read* 258). John Sepich rightly points out that the description of the Judge as a "vast abhorrence" (McCarthy 243) suggests, etymologically, his destructive potential: "'vast' out of the Latin *'vastus* void, of immense size, extent,' but as a verb, meaning 'to lay waste, destroy'; an 'abhorrence is 'a horror to cause trembling' (*OED*)" (Sepich 139). We might also keep in mind here the conceptual correspon-dence between the name Holden and several senses of the Greek verb *nemo*: the Judge is brutally preoccupied with the possession, control, and meting out of his own justice in wild (quasi-pastoral) places; engages in the fiery consumption of material and human presences; and feeds upon the land like some kind of anthropomorphized ulcer. Jefferson's "sacred fire," preserved in those who "labour in the earth" as "the chosen people of God" (Jefferson, *Notes* 290) becomes here a global scourge, for the Judge, as Hesiod notes of Prometheus, "lovingly embrac[es]" fire (*Works and Days* 55), that consumptive power "which does contain within it," McCarthy's narrator insists, "something of men themselves" (McCarthy 244).

The title of McCarthy's novel offers further clues to the qualities inher-ent in the Judge's ruthless bloodletting and scorching of the land. Merid-ian can mean "a graduated ring or half-ring within which an artificial globe is suspended and revolves concentrically" (*OED*), a dramatic and fitting image of the earthly control sought by the Judge as suzerain. The Judge might also be thought of as illustrating another sense of meridian, "a notional line on the surface of a spherical or other curved body, esp. the eyeball, analogous to or resembling a terrestrial meridian" (*OED*), which adds to Emerson's famous image of augmented personal vision a sugges-tion of cartographical mastery. In his adversarial relationship to every-thing beyond himself, the Judge assumes the role of Satan, "the Adversary" (in Hebrew, "*ha'satan*"), for whom meridian is in fact a proper name: the thirteenth-century manual *Ancrene Riwle* offers the warning "kepe hym þan from meridiane þe deuel" (*OED*), taking its cue from Psalm 91:6, "the destruction *that* wasteth at noonday." Meridian can also refer to the quiddity of something, its discrete whatness: "A locality, situation, or constituency considered as separate and distinct from others, and as having its own particular character; the special character or circumstances by which one place, person, set of persons, etc., is distinguished from others" (*OED*). In this sense, the Judge seeks (bloodily) his ultimate meridian, a full separation from other presences, an utter self-definition or self-pasture, figuratively rendered in the appearance of a thing, shadowless and so wholly itself, as the sun is directly overhead. A member of the Glanton gang named Tobin describes the Judge at midday, perched, appropriately, on a *boundary* stone: "Then about the meridian of that day we come upon the judge on his rock there in that wilderness by his single self. Aye and there was no rock, just the one. Irving said he'd brung it with him. I said that it was a merestone for to mark him out of nothing at all" (McCarthy 125). This stone is a punning *mere*-idian: "mere" as a noun can mean "boundary," and as an adjective, "pure, unmixed, unalloyed; undiluted, unadulterated" (*OED*). Rhetorical and philosophical connections with Nietzsche's Zarathustra seem overt here: in chapter 10 of part 4, "At Midday," the self-mastering Übermensch rests under the noon sun—yet another sense of meridian, "A rest taken at or around midday; a siesta" (*OED*)—"and in falling asleep Zarathustra spoke thus to his heart: 'Still! Still! Did the world not just become perfect?" (Nietzsche, *Thus Spake* 240–41; Graham Parkes translation). The figurative sense of meridian which denotes a climax of powers—"The point or period of highest development or perfection, after which decline sets in; culmination, full splendor" (*OED*)—is also especially evocative of the Judge, who uses the word in this sense himself: "The way of the world is to bloom and to flower and die but in the affairs of men there is no waning and the noon of his expression signals the onset of night. His spirit is exhausted at the peak of its achievement. His meridian is at once his darkening and the evening of his day. He loves games? Let him play for stakes. This you see here, these ruins wondered at by tribes of savages, do you not think that this will be again? Aye. And again. With other people, with other sons" (McCarthy 146–47). These other "sons" are, perhaps, also other "suns." Once one's meridian has been achieved, says the Judge, no further development is possible—growth ends and darkness falls after the perfection of self-pasture, a movement repeated endlessly through history, and echoed in Nietzsche's notion of eternal recurrence.[1]

McCarthy's "Evening Redness in the West" proffers a version of identification with Nature and the radical even-ing of human and natural things that is, needless to say, much less friendly than Emerson's: "here [in the desert] was nothing more luminous than another and nothing more enshadowed and in the optical democracy of such landscapes all preference is made whimsical and a man and a rock become endowed with unguessed kinships" (McCarthy 247). The Judge sees *nomos* as an illegitimate restraint on the strong, a mask for the predatory realities of what Callicles called "the law of nature" and for what he subsumes under the rubric of "history": "Moral law is an invention of mankind for the disenfranchisement of the powerful in favor of the weak. Historical law subverts it at every turn" (250). As an earthly suzerain, he vastly inflates both Callicles's and Emerson's claims, effectively conflating human and divine law (*nomos* and *themis*) in the self-lawed—*autonomos*—person. There is no genuine law, the Judge would insist, other than unrestrained predation. In a rather different manner than Callicles, however, the Judge treats this law as if it had the binding force of *themis*: he is *fanatically* committed to worshiping *physis* as a god and fully realizing his all-consuming selfhood, whereas the Greek amoralist (from the limited evidence we have in the *Gorgias*) seems merely cynical. The Judge is, in this respect, kin to both Antigone and Socrates, who similarly pledge themselves to their conception of themistic authority.

Emerson's faith in the power of vision (and a language based on that vision) posits no limit to what can be subordinated to human purposes: "There is no object so foul that intense light will not make beautiful. And the stimulus it affords to the sense, and a sort of infinitude which it hath, like space and time, make all matter gay. Even the corpse has its own beauty" (Emerson, *Nature* 9). The Judge sees ample beauty in corpses, which are often attractively described in the novel (the beauty here, I take it, is McCarthy's ironic rendering of the *Judge*'s vision, or in other words a representation of the terrible beauty of the American sublime): "All about her the dead lay with their peeled skulls like polyps bluely wet or luminescent melons cooling on some mesa of the moon. In the days to come the frail black rebuses of blood in those sands would crack and break and drift away so that in the circuit of few suns all trace of the destruction of these people would be erased. The desert wind would salt their ruins and there would be nothing, nor ghost nor scribe, to tell to any pilgrim in his passing how it was that people had lived in this place and in this place died" (McCarthy 174). Emerson seeks God in a matching of vision and language, a harmonizing of the infinite vitality of the natural world with the human potential for vivifying speech from dead metaphor: "But wise men pierce this rotten diction and fasten words again to visible things; so that picturesque language is at once a commanding certificate that he who employs it is a man in alliance with truth and God" (Emerson, *Nature* 16). The Judge, too, sees language as potentially harmonized with the visible—"Words are things" (McCarthy 85)—but employs speech as merely another type of war, a means to deceive, dominate, and destroy those who would listen to him. God "speaks in stones and trees, the bones of things" (116), he declaims, but since the divine is synonymous with warfare, all aspects of the natural world become rivals which "can enslave man" (198) if they are not aggressively countered. Intent on hunting down "Whatever in creation exists without [his] knowledge" (198), the Judge destroys material things (humans, animals, artifacts, etc.) in his quest to know and absorb the world, and thus tilts the productive and emancipating potential of Emerson's trope toward (but not yet reaching) a singularity composed of nothing *but* the mastering, self-pastured self, pasturing *on* itself.

Throughout *Nature,* Emerson insists on the importance of forging "an original relation to the universe" (*Nature* 3) so that one might "Build therefore [one's] own world" (39). Such originality, according to Emerson, negates age and historical indebtedness, for "In the woods is perpetual youth" (6). McCarthy's treatment of the Judge ferociously ironizes the productive potential of this sort of world building (as well as implicitly critiquing Mailer's faith in the creative potential of human regression), and his defiance of time is reflected in his appearance: particularly devoted to preying on children, he seems, in fact, to be regenerated by their blood, looking himself like an overgrown baby with his bald head, "oddly childish lips" (McCarthy 140), and small hands and feet. In his story of the harnessmaker, the Judge baroquely underscores the significance of claiming liberty from paternal authority, framing this challenge in Oedipal terms as he describes the fate of sons who do not slay their fathers: "Now this son whose father's existence in this world is historical and speculative even before the son has entered it is in a bad way. All his life he carries before him the idol of a perfection to which he can never attain. The father dead has euchered the son out of his patrimony" (145). Hostile to all priority, the Judge seems to represent the wholly triumphant "son" in such a dynamic. As Tobin remarks of him: "You couldnt tell where he'd come from. Said he'd been with a wagon company and fell out to go it alone" (125). This obscuring of origins is further developed in the narrative's description of the kid's dream, which renders the Judge as finally unreadable and unknowable: "Whoever would seek out his history through what unraveling of loins and ledgerbooks must stand at last darkened and dumb at the shore of a void without terminus or origin and whatever science he might bring to bear upon the dusty primal matter blowing down out of the millennia will discover no trace of any ultimate atavistic egg by which to reckon his commencing" (309–10).

Blood Meridian presents the Judge as plausibly and continually "self-rebegotten," for he is not just without origin but able to make and remake himself, assuming convenient disguises and employing a silver tongue with Odyssean skill. He contains any number of contradictions—dancer and destroyer, scholar and soldier, father and child—and his ability to assume multiple roles is crucial to his dominance: he can fit in anywhere, temporarily adopting and exploiting the various cliques he joins, in order to advance his suzerainty. Though bent on destruction and finally monomaniacal, he has a joyfulness missing in Ahab: it is sheer pleasure for the Judge to follow his God. However, his multiplicity ought also to be thought of as emblematic of a deliberate *refusal* to commit to any social role, to submit to a place within a community and its laws at the expense of nurturing the infinite possibilities of his own autonomy. Quentin Anderson's formulation of the American "secular incarnation" (a "catching up of all [the father's] powers into the self," which forms the basis of what he calls the "imperial self") is uncannily suggestive of the Judge's refusal and its relation to his absorptive project: "It was this inclusive fantasy from which Emerson fell back in later years, but he never found anything satisfactory to take its place, either in the 'conduct of life' or any lesser formula. Nor could he take it back. For him, and for us, the failure of the fathers proved definitive" (Anderson 58). Exceeding Emerson's "catching up" of paternal power, the Judge, paranoically hostile to all rivals, would contain and destroy them as he becomes his own father, radically autonomous. He cannot recruit the kid, though he seems to try, and therefore will not (and, of course, seemingly does not need to) re-create himself through an heir. Indeed, any leadership the Judge offers is profoundly ambivalent, since his prime lesson is that one must not accept external authorities. When the Judge lectures his companions, establishing his own authority in all earthly matters, he mocks those who would give up their own quest for autonomy by believing him: "The squatters in their rags nodded among themselves and were soon reckoning him correct, this man of learning, in all his speculation, and this the judge encouraged until they were right proselytes of the new order whereupon he laughed at them for fools" (McCarthy 116). No community, no submission to social roles and nomistic ties, can coexist with the demands of such autonomy.

Blood Meridian thus insists on how "very expensive [a] torso" such an American sublime could be when autonomous persons confront the material world. The Judge proffers an incendiary version of the American sublime as he approaches its meridian—Bloom's "solitude and the abyss"—desolating whatever stands before him as he seeks to "expunge . . . from the memory of man" (140) all traces of the human and natural past. The Judge and Glanton gang, laying waste to the Southwest, also recover here the destructive senses of *nemo* (in a memorable line, McCarthy suggests the pathological quality of American expansion in his description of an anonymous group of "goldseekers" as "Itinerant degenerates bleeding westward like some heliotropic plague" [78]). However, while Homer may sing of individuals, peoples, even whole city-states burnt away, he does not, as McCarthy does here, go so far as to hint at the *earth itself* being wholly mastered or consumed by human efforts, or the emergence of autonomous persons—nomads (from *nomos* as "pasture") of the American meridian—who might carry out such a hyperbolic project. The Judge's fiery, pathological march across the land acknowledges no limit to the exercise of martial power, no external law to inhibit him beyond his version of *physis*, the ostensibly divine law of endless warfare itself.

Needless to say, such a stance poses extreme hazards to the powerless. Human devastation is suggested in *Blood Meridian*'s overwhelming inventory of casualties—its slaughtered villages, trees of dead babies, and corpse-dotted deserts—with Native Americans, the object of the Glanton gang's scalp-hunting mission, taking the brunt of the carnage. Where Emerson saw the natural world as an infinite resource always dwarfing any products of its human exploitation—our "operations taken together are so insignificant, a little chipping, baking, patching, and washing, that in an impression so grand as that of the world on the human mind, they do not vary the result" (*Nature* 4)—McCarthy prophesies Nature's end after its exhaustion by the human will. R. W. B. Lewis's analysis of the pyrolytic inclinations of the archetype he dubbed the "American Adam" identifies such destructiveness as inherent in the American imagination of autonomy. Lewis's discussion of Hawthorne's "Earth's Holocaust," which he calls "truer than history," notes how a crowd feeds an enormous and all-consuming bonfire with symbols of the past in order to destroy historical debt: "Hawthorne, as usual, enlarged upon his historical materials; and, in doing so, he managed very accurately to catch in a fable the prevailing impulse to escape from every existing mode of organizing and explaining experience, in order to confront life in entirely original terms. And at the same time, in the divided attitude that gives his story its vital tension, Hawthorne managed to convey the deep reservations that certain Americans felt about the contemporary passion to destroy" (Lewis 14). President Andrew Jackson's orchestration of Indian removal—which belongs to an ideological enterprise similar to the Judge's—furnishes another vivid illustration of the consumptive forces described in McCarthy's novel. Michael Paul Rogin robustly summarizes the president's decrees, noting Jackson's "infantile" characteristics which further reinforce a connection with the Judge: "Jackson returned to childhood in nature, not as a lover of nature, but to sanctify possessions and dominate childhood. The American Indians, wrote Thoreau, burned their possessions in a yearly ritual of purification. Jackson's life was purifying too; as his friend Judge John Catron eulogized him, he burned everything before him like a prairie fire. The spirit of infancy he retained into manhood was the spirit of infantile rage" (Rogin 37).

In a scene emphasizing his role as *meridiane þe deuel*, the Judge walks through fire, looking "like a great ponderous djinn," "the flames deliver[ing] him up as if he were in some way native to their element" (McCarthy 96). Part of the Judge's destructive enterprise involves collecting historical objects and then ritualistically committing them to the nightly bonfire: "Then he sat with his hands cupped in his lap and he seemed much satisfied with the world, as if his counsel had been sought at its creation" (140). In one of the most dramatic passages of the novel, Tobin describes the Judge's concoction of a mysterious gunpowder which allows the men to commit "a slaughter of the aborigines" (122):

> God it was a butchery. At the first fire we killed a round dozen and we did not let up. Before the last poor nigger reached the bottom of the slope there was fifty-eight of them lay slaughtered among the gravels. They just slid down the slope like chaff down a hopper, some turned this way, some that, and they made a chain about the base of the mountain. We rested our rifle barrels on the brimstone and we shot nine more on the lava where they ran. It was a stand, what it was. Wagers was laid. The last of them shot was a reckonable part of a mile from the muzzles of the guns and that on a dead run. It was sharp shootin all around and not a misfire in the batch of that queer powder. (134)

After Tobin tells the story of the gunpowder, the kid twice asks of the Judge, "What's he a judge of?" (135). Tobin does not answer the question, instead "[glancing] off across the fire" (135), but might as well have replied that the Judge is the fiery climax of American sublimity, the autonomous angel of the apocalypse, who seeks to clear away, consuming in a terminal conflagration, all the world before him.

The exterminations carried out by the Judge and the Glanton gang vividly suggest the environmental ruin produced by this mode of American sublimity. The predatory ethos, sustainable by small numbers in large spaces, becomes fantastically destructive, McCarthy suggests, once its adherents join together: "For although each man among them was discrete unto himself, conjoined they made a thing that had not been before and in that communal soul were wastes hardly reckonable more than those whited regions on old maps where monsters do live and where there is nothing other of the known world save conjectural winds" (152). Mental voids are inevitably materialized, as is made clear in a passage near the novel's end, where an aged hunter tells of the rapid extinction of buffalo brought on by unrestrained human predation: "We ransacked the country. Six weeks. Finally found a herd of eight animals and we killed them and come in. They're gone. Ever one of them that God ever made is gone as if they'd never been at all" (317). Compare here the description of natural fecundity—the teeming pasture greeting the newly arrived hunter—by Filson's Daniel Boone: "We found every where abundance of wild beasts of all sorts, through this vast forest. The buffaloes were more frequent than I have seen cattle in the settlements, browzing on the leaves of the cane, or croping the herbage on those extensive plains, fearless, because ignorant, of the violence of man. Sometimes we saw hundreds in a drove, and the numbers about the salt springs were amazing. In this forest, the habitation of beasts of every kind natural to America, we practised hunting with great success" (Filson 40–41). At its logical endpoint the version of American sublimity depicted by McCarthy would dominate and empty the world, with the Judge and his exemplars at last a law, but also a pasture, unto themselves.

Early in *Blood Meridian*, Captain White, the leader of a doomed filibustering expedition against Mexico, seduces the kid into joining him with a promise of a pasture of his own: "There will be a section of land for every man in my company. Fine grassland. Some of the finest in the world. A land rich in minerals, in gold and silver I would say beyond the wildest speculation" (McCarthy 34). White ends with his severed head preserved in a jar, while the kid is murdered by the Judge in an outhouse—both deaths emblematic, as was Antigone's, of miserably shrunken space or bathetic self-pasturing. The novel concludes, some three decades after the

Glanton gang's exploits, with America's continental expansion complete, its Native American population brutally decimated, and its frontier, as Frederick Jackson Turner would frame it in 1893, all but "closed." Nevertheless, we are led to suspect that the seductive power of the American sublime remains, though straightforwardly violent expressions of it will necessarily be more complicated. As the Judge pronounces:

> I tell you this. As war becomes dishonored and its nobility called into question those honorable men who recognize the sanctity of blood will become excluded from the dance, which is the warrior's right, and thereby will the dance become a false dance and the dancers false dancers. And yet there will be one there always who is a true dancer and can you guess who that might be? . . . Only that man who has offered up himself entire to the blood of war, who has been to the floor of the pit and seen horror in the round and learned at last that it speaks to his inmost heart, only that man can dance. (331)

McCarthy's Judge, in implicating the American sublime in horrific actualities, exposes the aggressive potential in Emersonian identification with the land and the consumptive terrors of self-lawed persons. The novel's cryptic epilogue goes further in suggesting, through its description of Promethean fence builders who "strike fire in the hole" and seek "the verification of a principle, a validation of sequence and causality" (337), not just the formal rationalization of the land which followed the closing of the frontier, but also the psychologically and materially constricted conditions under which American sublimity would endure in the nation. What the Judge calls "True dancers," implies McCarthy, do not disappear after the nineteenth century. These devotees of *physis*, exuberant heirs to Callicles in an age even more corrosive to the communal ties of *nomos*, will merely operate in more tightly bound spaces, harried and inward-turning, nomads of the meridian's evening, hyperautonomous, in fatal pursuit of limitless self-pasture.

7 / Hyperautonomy

> *The ambiguity and ambivalence of American individualism derive from both cultural and social contradictions. We insist, perhaps more than ever before, on finding our true selves independent of any cultural or social influence, being responsible to that self alone, and making its fulfillment the very meaning of our lives. Yet we spend much of our time navigating through immense bureaucratic structures—multiversities, corporations, government agencies—manipulating and being manipulated by others.*
>
> —ROBERT N. BELLAH ET AL., *HABITS OF THE HEART: INDIVIDUALISM AND COMMITMENT IN AMERICAN LIFE*

Don DeLillo's work exemplifies the lingering, postmeridial undeath of personal autonomy. In it we find anatomized the concept I call *hyper*autonomy, an augmentation of the self so great, an opening of possibilities so absolute, that what begins in the nation's (literary and cultural) history as a liberty that *fulfills* the self, ends in a paradoxical and pathological *emptying*—first of any meaningful and sustainable relationship between individual and community, and finally of any sense of individuality itself.

The pastoral world Jefferson describes, through which the divine and its laws can be known, disappears here with the collapse of Nature into the human. This late stage of autonomy hyperbolizes Tocqueville's observation in 1840 about the American self's isolation—"Everyone shuts himself up in his own breast, and affects from that point to judge the world" (Tocqueville 2.1.1.512)—and its paradoxical vulnerability to social conformity: "Not only is common opinion the only guide which private judgment retains amongst a democratic people, but amongst such a people it possesses a power infinitely beyond what it has elsewhere" (2.1.2.519). Liberated from binding obligations to the human *nomos*, and yet inevitably located within its now universal sprawl, the hyperautonomist begins to pasture freely, in a self-terminating pathology, on nomistic mediations. Where the ancient Greeks contrasted *themis* (divine, eternal, *unwritten* law) with humanly constructed law, for DeLillo's America "the laws of Nature and of Nature's God" have been rewritten as human derivatives. The hyperautonomists in DeLillo still claim a morbidly attenuated version of that solitary access to themistic authority bequeathed them by the

Transcendentalists, and with it the supreme authority to judge and sentence the human *nomos*, but their transgressive acts—characteristically suggestive of a grotesque parody of the mythic frontiersman's sacred predation—finally amount to a radical, self-effacing implication in simulative and *un*regenerative violence. Radical autonomy reaches its vanishing point here: a self-pasture that is, at last, a pasturing *on* the self, a self-consuming and self-consumed nomadism. In the perfect singularity of the hyperautonomist's self-possession, the Judge's fierce meridian selfhood is finally exhausted and collapses into itself, becoming a kind of black hole in nomistic space, feeding endlessly on the human world around it. The hyperautonomous self is dissolved into that world, a transparent and impersonal eyeball as *nothing* (and everything). Personal auto-nomy comes to suggest, at last, a kind of auto-matic role-playing, with the person—or rather the original *persona*, but without the speaker speaking through—nothing but a mutable mask, assimilated into the machinal processes of its own celebration.

DeLillo's *White Noise* (1985), *Libra* (1988), and *Underworld* (1997) limn hyperautonomy in contemporary America, while also tacitly revising Mailer's endorsement of Romantic faith and frontier heroism in urban, commercial environments. *DeLillo's* "white negroes" turn inward, as neo-Transcendentalists, to the infinite spaces of mass mediation, and outward, as urban frontiersman, to futile acts of violent release, transforming Bumppo and Boone's sacred hunting grounds into a sterile and solipsistic *dys*nomia. *White Noise* charts the territory of self-pasture—a residual "Nature" and *themis* now interfused with the artificial—in late-twentieth-century, consumerist America, where Epicurean ideals reemerge in ironic and wretchedly desperate forms, undead. *Libra* and *Underworld*, in the figures of Lee Harvey Oswald and Richard Henry Gilkey, present two quintessential hyperautonomists who inhabit that territory, isolate killers who contain, and are contained by, the worlds around them.

In Mailer's *The Naked and the Dead*, the fascistic General Cummings lauds Hitler's political rise in the 1930s: "I tell you that [he] is not a flash in the pan. . . . He has the germ of an idea, and moreover you've got to give him political credit. He plays on the German people with consummate skill. That Siegfried business is fundamental to them" (*Naked* 367). Mailer would later invoke the specter of Hitler, in tandem with the prospect of nuclear annihilation, in the first sentence of "The White Negro": "Probably, we will never be able to determine the psychic havoc of the concentration camps and the atom bomb upon the unconscious mind of almost everyone alive in these years" ("White Negro" 311). Totalitarianism and organized mass death are, for Mailer, the ineluctable conditions of modernity, resulting in the suffocation of personal autonomy and the state-sponsored imposition of a cowardly conformity: "A stench of fear has come out of every pore of American life, and we suffer from a collective failure of nerve. The only courage, with rare exceptions, . . . has been the isolated courage of isolated people" (312).

White Noise implicitly engages Mailer's thesis in 1980s America. The narrator of this satirical novel, Jack Gladney, "chairman of the department of Hitler studies at the College-on-the-Hill" (*White Noise* 4), is obsessed by the prospect of dying in a routine, anonymous fashion— that is, in a way similar to those in the Nazis' concentration camps, who are, tellingly, never invoked in the book. As Gladney's colleague, Murray Jay Siskind, remarks of urban anonymity: "In cities no one notices specific dying. Dying is a quality of the air. It's everywhere and nowhere. Men shout as they die, to be noticed, remembered for a second or two" (38). Gladney navigates an environment in which abundant consumer choices coexist with the ubiquitous manipulations of corporate powers—Mailer's "totalitarianism"—and their potential to extinguish vulnerable individuals. Where Boone and Bumppo might hope for death on the sacred hunt, just after an *aristeia* in which they fulfill their human promise, Gladney is uncertain of the terms of the sacred or of human excellence. His cultivation of pleasure and a satisfying private life (in place of broader political commitments) makes him something like a modern, rather desperate Epicurean, though one whose careful hedonism only seems to exacerbate fears of death. *Ataraxia* (tranquility) and *aponia* (freedom from pain) are, for him, coveted but elusive ideals.

The novel begins with a description of the first day of school at Gladney's university, its opening sentence a parody of frontier expansion: "The station *wagons* arrived at noon, a long shining line that coursed through the *west* campus" (3; italics added). These wagons bring an endless diversity of consumer goods to this academic outpost, and they play a key role in identity-formation: "This assembly of station wagons, as much as anything they might do in the course of the year, more than formal liturgies or laws, tells the parents they are a collection of the like-minded and the spiritually akin, a nation" (3–4). In this new "west," Americans pursue their happiness within a consumption-driven technological culture, committed to pleasure but harried by potent anxieties which seem to grow in tandem with consumer choices.

Whitman's celebration of erotic expression, implicitly endorsed in Mailer's philosophy of Hip and turn to the unconscious as "Nature," devolves here into a profusion of spiritually barren, hypermediated, finally unstimulating options. The empty liberation of the erotic self, able to feast on whatever it likes but no longer nourished by anything, is illustrated in a scene in which Gladney and his wife, Babette, attempt to titillate each other by reading from a smorgasbord of pornographic tales: "Pick your century. Do you want to read about Etruscan slave girls, Georgian rakes? I think we have some literature on flagellation brothels. What about the Middle Ages? We have incubi and succubi. Nuns galore" (29). Murray's willingness to discuss his erotic fantasies publicly and casually implies, moreover, a dilution of the importance of sex: as an imaginative category, it emerges without distinction among other secular topics, with sexual choice essentially no different than other consumer choices made within a free market: "One of [the prostitutes Murray has been talking to] is dressed in leopard loungewear under her coat. She showed me. Another one says she has a snap-off crotch. What do you think she means by that? I'm a little worried, though, about all these outbreaks of life-style diseases. I carry a reinforced ribbed condom at all times. One size fits all" (149). Suggesting, perhaps, the logical, dismal conclusion of liberal permissiveness about sex and an endorsement of anything "natural," Gladney's teenage son, Heinrich, casually remarks in a phone conversation: "Animals commit incest all the time. How unnatural can it be?" (34).

Racial otherness is also absorbed into mere "market diversity." Gladney is alarmed by America's changing racial demographics, particularly when he feels incapable of categorizing the racial others he sees. Mailer's invigorating binary of white and black—and its precursor, Bumppo and Boone's white "savagery"—effloresces here into a sort of infinite palette of racial and ethnic *différance*. Part of Gladney's obsession with Hitler derives, of course, from his concern for preserving "whiteness" and the illusions of personal autonomy it might provide. Tim Engles, reading *White Noise* "as a novel about the noise that white people make" (Engles 755), cogently demonstrates the connections DeLillo makes between threats to personal autonomy and the changing racial makeup of America. Gladney's status as a member of the white majority makes him "susceptible" (758), as Engles puts it, to believing in American self-reliance. Gladney's encounters with racialized others undermine that belief in a privileged status, suggesting to him that he is, like the "black man," a member of a group ("white men") with a particular, nomistically dependent set of features and standardized identity.

Intimations of the divine are common in DeLillo's technocratic America, but communion with *themis* tends to be trivial, idiosyncratic, and inevitably implicated in human origins, no matter how shadowy, rather than eternal and divine law. Babette reads various tabloids to an elderly man who "demands his weekly dose of cult mysteries" (5). Murray expounds on the mysticism of the supermarket —"'Everything is concealed in symbolism, hidden by veils of mystery and layers of cultural material'" (37)—and of television—"'The medium practically overflows with sacred formulas if we can remember how to respond innocently and get past our irritation, weariness and disgust'" (51). Flooded by disturbing but unreliable information from the media after an industrial accident releases a toxic substance, Jack and his family "[begin] to marvel at [their] own ability to manufacture awe" (153).

Institutional networks of power, panopticism, and cognitive conditioning are, as in Mailer, a preoccupying locus of speculation, and espionage has its place here, too: like Stephen Rojack's wife, Deborah, Jack's ex-wives have "ties to the intelligence community" (6). Gladney gauges the extent of corporate mind control when he hears his daughter, Steffie, repeat the words "Toyota Celica" in her sleep: "The utterance was beautiful and mysterious, gold-shot with looming wonder. It was like the name of an ancient power in the sky, tablet-carved in cuneiform. . . . Part of every child's brain noise, the substatic regions too deep to probe. Whatever its source, the utterance struck me with the import of a moment of splendid transcendence" (155). The "substatic regions" which create the "splendid transcendence" may be "too deep to probe," but they have their source, wherever it is, not in an externally located *themis* but rather in some human agency. Gladney's "splendid transcendence" involves an awareness of the (clearly meretricious) promise of consumer culture to overcome the isolation of the self through an awe-inspiring brand consciousness, a communality of consumption. The "ancient power in the sky" of the contemporary shopper's world is *not* supernatural or somehow beyond the human sphere, dwarfing the quotidian, but instead a product of human products, a projection, into the infinite, of human agency.

Emerson's and Thoreau's sense of Nature as distinct from the nomistic world, and yet potentially the source of its revitalization, becomes nonsensical here. "Natural" spectacles are associated in the novel with the corrupting human touch, as in the local sunsets Gladney admires which have "become almost unbearably beautiful" (170) since an industrial accident released a rare chemical into the air. Gladney's son, Heinrich, feels that "there's something ominous in the modern sunset," and near the end of the novel, Gladney describes the reactions of others who gaze at them: "The sky takes on content, feeling, an exalted narrative life. The bands of color reach so high, seem at times to separate into their constituent parts. There are turreted skies, light storms, softly falling streamers. It is hard to know how we should feel about this" (324). Not knowing exactly how to feel about what one sees is typical of DeLillo's characters. Natural beauty is hyperbolized and *de*natured here: a sunset becomes overwhelming in its apocalyptic portents, while the poisonous human interference implicated in the breathtaking "natural scene" serves as a reminder of the toxicity of the intoxicating sublime. One of DeLillo's literary disciples, Bret Easton Ellis, provocatively echoes this scene in *American Psycho* (1991): Patrick Bateman, the novel's homicidal narrator, hyperbolizes Jack's thoughts on the deadliness of sunsets and their implication in consumer culture in a gory contemplation of urban clouds: "I see [in the sky . . .] a Gucci money clip, an ax, a woman cut in two, a large puffy white puddle of blood that spreads across the sky, dripping over the city, onto Manhattan" (Ellis 371). For DeLillo and Ellis, one encounters an *urbs naturae* implicated in, and threatening the extinction of, all human interests.

To consume in America is, the novel suggests, to partake in the illusion of overcoming death by encountering a seemingly endless supply and variety of things: endless shopping aisles, endless goods, endless television, all of which promise an endlessly consuming self, immortally seeking and acquiring. Insulted by a colleague, Gladney goes shopping in order to restore a sense of "endless well-being" (83), finding, in what Jean Baudrillard calls the "primary landscape [le paysage]" of Western affluence, "the final and magical negation of scarcity [. . . , which] mimic[s] a new-found nature of prodigious fecundity" (Baudrillard 30). Gladney knows, however, that consumer culture can only repress the fear of death in its suggestion of endlessness, offering the aura of immortality while generating its own forms of death and corruption. Told by doctors that his exposure to an "airborne toxic event" will likely kill him *some day*, though it is not clear when, he turns wildly against his own consumption, throwing away (some of) his material possessions in an attempt to challenge his fear. As Murray notes in his lectures, death is vigorously repressed in consumer culture, "But it continues to grow, to acquire breadth and scope, new outlets, new passages and means. The more we learn, the more it grows" (150).

For DeLillo's characters, death is merely a source of anxiety—rather than, as for Bumppo and Boone, a vivifying existential provocation—and responses to it are both extreme and (self-)destructive. Babette seeks out the rogue scientist Willie Mink and the experimental drug Dylar in order to overcome her death fears, while Orest Mercator, a teenage friend of Gladney's son, Heinrich, plans to confront his own mortality by sitting in a room full of poisonous snakes, thus making it possible to "leap free of everyday dying" (267). Heinrich, precociously articulate and attuned to the inauthentic, ominously dons a "camouflage jacket and cap" (109) that suggest his status as a kind of urban frontiersman manqué. Babette fears that the boy may have the potential for violence—acted out, of course, according to lurid cultural clichés: "[She] is afraid he will end up in a barricaded room, spraying hundreds of rounds of automatic fire across an empty mall before the SWAT teams come for him with their heavy-barreled weapons, their bullhorns and body armor" (22). Heinrich worries his father by playing chess by mail with a mass murderer named Tommy Roy Foster, and Jack's concerned questioning of his son exposes the extent to which the killer's role has begun to seem *merely* a (prescripted) *persona*, losing its potential for idiosyncratic expression and nomistic critique:

> "Who did he kill?"
> "He was under pressure."
> "And what happened?"
> "It kept building and building."
> "So he went out and shot someone. Who did he shoot?"
> "Some people in Iron City."
> "How many?"
> "Five."
> "Five people."
> "Not counting the state trooper, which was later."
> "Six people. Did he care for his weapons obsessively? Did he have an arsenal stashed in his shabby little room off a six-story concrete car park?"
> "Some handguns and a bolt-action rifle with a scope."
> "A telescopic sight. Did he fire from a highway overpass, a rented room? Did he walk into a bar, a washette, his former place of employment and start firing indiscriminately? People scattering, taking cover under tables. People out on the street thinking they heard firecrackers. 'I was just waiting for the bus when I heard this little popping noise like firecrackers going off.'"
> "He went up to a roof."

"A rooftop sniper. Did he write in his diary before he went up
to the roof? Did he make tapes of his voice, go to the movies, read
books about other mass murderers to refresh his memory?" (44)

Gladney mocks these clichéd particulars, while Heinrich notes that
Foster would have acted with an eye to larger celebrity if given another
chance: "He says if he had to do it all over again, he wouldn't do it as
an ordinary murder, he would do it as an assassination" (45). What this
aspirant to infamy might have been, to himself and to the jaded public encountering his mass-mediated persona, is always already a hoary
formula. The agency of the contemporary killer is, moreover, imperiled along with his individuality. Heinrich, playing a radical skepticism
against his father's desperate need for belief, echoes Epicurus's atomist
philosophy in alluding to the scientific reduction of all human action
to material forces: "I can't control what happens in my brain, so how
can I be sure what I want to do ten seconds from now, much less Mon-
tana next summer? It's all this activity in the brain and you don't know
what's you as a person and what's some neuron that just happens to
fire or just happens to misfire. Isn't that why Tommy Roy killed those
people?" (45–46).

A number of characters in *White Noise* who do not commit violent
crimes still dream of doing so, as if in (at least partial) confirmation
of Robert Warshow's remark that the film gangster represents "what
we want to be and what we are afraid we may become" (Warshow 131).
A colleague of Gladney's solemnly cites "Richard Widmark in *Kiss of
Death*" as the greatest influence on his life: "'When [he] pushed that old
lady in that wheelchair down that flight of stairs, it was like a personal
breakthrough for me'" (214–15). The comic moment reinforces the novel's
insistence on the self's absorption, and hackneyed reprisal, of mediated
personae. One finds one's sense of self onscreen, DeLillo suggests, and
cinematic possibilities are acted out with wildly destructive results.
Gladney's own decision to commit murder is fuelled by Murray, who
focuses his rage using an assortment of motifs drawn from the mythic
frontiersman's legacy in cowboy and gangster films: "'Nothingness is
staring you in the face. Utter and permanent oblivion. You will cease to
be, Jack. The dier accepts this and dies. The killer, in theory, attempts to
defeat his own death by killing others. He buys time, he buys life. Watch
others squirm. See the blood in the dust'" (291).

White Noise climaxes with a parody of frontier violence. Setting
out to avenge himself as a cuckold, Gladney momentarily feels himself

achieving, at last, a profound and self-augmenting nomistic detachment: "I ran a red light when I crossed Middlebrook. Reaching the end of the expressway ramp, I did not yield. All the way to Iron City I felt a sense of dreaminess, release, unreality" (302). His heightened state holds, as it did for Stephen Rojack—who claims after killing his wife that his "flesh seemed new" (Mailer, *American Dream* 36)—the promise of rebirth into an autonomous selfhood. Shooting Willie Mink, Gladney claims: "I knew who I was in the network of meanings. Water fell to earth in drops, causing surfaces to gleam. I saw things new" (312). But Gladney in fact casts himself here in cinematic clichés, from his intention to shoot Mink "three times in the viscera for maximum pain," to his plan, voiced several times, to "walk home in the rain and the fog" (304). Instead of encountering a worthy and dignified "savage" who might pass on his strength before dying, Gladney meets a pathetic automaton—the epitome of hyperautonomy—who mouths clichés from television dialogue: "Why are you here, white man?" (310). Gladney does not receive from his vanquished opponent a new name authenticating his entry into "Nature," like Bumppo in *Deerslayer,* and the absurd confrontation allows for no regenerative violence of the type identified by Slotkin as the mythical outcome of frontier experience. Though Gladney has risked danger in acting antisocially, he has not, finally, "dared the unknown" like Mailer's "eighteen-year-old hoodlums" who "beat in the brains of a candy-store keeper" ("White Negro" 321). The script is pre- and overdetermined, the performance merely a reiteration of stock conventions. After shooting Mink and being shot himself, Gladney abandons the role of assassin for that of liberator in a captivity narrative, dragging a wounded man to safety: "Having shot him, having led him to believe he'd shot himself, I felt I did honor to both of us, to all of us, by merging our fortunes, physically leading him to safety" (315). The act lacks any potential for vital autonomous expression, and in spite of his efforts, Gladney finds himself still subject to, and indeed more deeply confirmed within, his trivializing and self-consumptive *nomos.*

The final paragraph of DeLillo's first novel, *Americana*, describes the narrator's retracing of Kennedy's fatal trip through Dallas, "past the School Book Depository, through Dealey Plaza and beneath the triple underpass . . . and out past Parkland Hospital" (388). Eight novels later, DeLillo's *Libra* returns us to the scene of the assassination, while deepening the author's engagement with what has remained his principal theme: the complicated status of personal autonomy in a landscape dominated by technology and the mediated image. Douglas Keesey conjectures that "DeLillo's main subject all along has been men in small rooms, and his unconscious model may well have been Oswald sitting in his prison cell after his arrest for Kennedy's assassination" (Keesey 151). Asked by a journalist whether he could have invented this event if it had not actually happened, DeLillo is quoted as replying: "Maybe it invented me" (DeCurtis 47).

In DeLillo, the vigorous autonomy identified by Mailer as beleaguered—but still possible for the heroic—is no longer available. The often frenzied search for it persists, however, as personal renewal remains a common obsession in spite of its habitual futility, breeding its own cast of violent aspirants to autonomy. Mailer's "white negro," whose purgative violence promised a more vital selfhood, yields in DeLillo to something like a raving everyman: deadly but ordinary, committed to action but finally void of higher purpose. As DeLillo's Nicholas Branch, the fictional researcher writing a "secret history" (*Libra* 15) of the Kennedy assassination, describes the uncanny commonness of the man in the pictures he examines: "Oswald even looks like different people from one photograph to the next. He is solid, frail, thin-lipped, broad-featured, extroverted, shy and bank-clerkish, all, with the columned neck of a fullback. He looks like everybody" (300). This failure of individuality suggests the vastly compromised status of American autonomy. Absent is the potential of Mailer's hipster, in love with movement and electrically alive in the present, to "make a little better nervous system" ("White Negro" 323) so that he might "[make] the new habit, unearthing the new talent which the old frustration denied" (324). DeLillo's Oswald may launch an impassioned nomistic critique—"[They're] always trying to sell you something. Everything is based on forcing people to buy. If you can't buy what they're selling, you're a zero in the system" (*Libra* 40)—but finally proffers no alternatives other than destructive acts of vengeance (performed, of course, according to formulas devised by others and in terms often suggestive of media clichés). In Oswald the desire for reinvention may endure, but it tends either to evaporate quickly when opposed by intractable barriers, or wash out toward oblivion over a floodplain of shallow possibilities.

Libra posits an assassination conspiracy that nominally places the blame for President Kennedy's murder on rogue elements in the CIA, but, more profoundly, suggests the culpability of the American *nomos* itself by sketching a citizenry deranged by a preoccupation with fantasy and mediated spectacles. We may never be able to identify the specific guilty parties, DeLillo implies, but we can understand in a broad sense the scene of the crime. A guilty verdict falls, ultimately, not on the CIA or on Oswald, but rather on the communal fascination with mediated images that has propelled both Kennedy's telegenic emergence and the lethal proclivities of his killer (or, for DeLillo, one of his killers). In this scheme (which contrasts with the "lone gunman" theory Mailer proposes in *Oswald's Tale* (1995)), Oswald is an eccentric, but in him we may locate the heart of America's nomistic pathology.

Libra gives us, in fact, a lone assassin invented through conspiracy, an "autonomous person" scripted not just by co-assassins, but by the contemporary American *nomos*. Long before his recruitment into the plot to kill Kennedy, DeLillo's Oswald reveals an affinity for ambitious— yet always thwarted—inward adventuring. As a youngster he immerses himself in books that offer relief from an unhappy life, his imagination transforming the familiarly wretched and trivial into the grandly historic: "He wanted subjects and ideas of historic scope, ideas that touched his life, his true life, the whirl of time inside him" (33). Oswald's relation to those ideas fails at what both Emerson and Thoreau suggest is the sine qua non of the American *idiotes*, an original relation to what one consumes intellectually, an ultimate detachment from one's influences. His reading (and consumption of other media) does not catalyze his own creative thinking, but instead tends merely to augment his own resentment and spawn vengeful fantasies. Vision, for Emerson the master metaphor of autonomy, symbolically weakens and darkens here in the form of severe dyslexia, a blindness isolating the self:

> Always the pain, the chaos of composition. He could not find order in the field of little symbols. They were in the hazy distance. . . .
> The nature of things was to be elusive. Things slipped through his perceptions. He could not get a grip on the runaway world.
> Limits everywhere. In every direction he came up against his own incompleteness. Cramped, fumbling, deficient. He knew things. It wasn't that he didn't know. (211)

Oswald's private experience remains private, for he cannot translate it to other selves—cannot heed Emerson's advice to "Build your own world" (*Nature* 39), or, as Win Everett says of the "Oswald" that the conspirators would construct, cannot "extend [his] fiction into the world" (*Libra* 50).

Though he would see himself as the equivalent of other revolutionaries—"Men in small rooms. Men reading and waiting, struggling with secret and feverish ideas." (41)—his nomistic detachment produces only a volatility and ductility in the Libran's scales, a susceptibility to being "tipped," according to some external influence, one way or another. DeLillo's Clay Shaw divides the Libran type into its positive and negative versions: the former has claimed both autonomy and a high public status—he "has achieved self-mastery. He is well balanced, levelheaded, a sensible fellow respected by all" (315)—while the latter is suggestive of hyperautonomy and its utter vulnerability to external authorities—he is "'somewhat unsteady and impulsive. Easily, easily, easily influenced. Poised to make the dangerous leap'" (315). As DeLillo's Ferrie notes, Oswald perfectly represents the negative Libran, a self large enough, like Whitman's speaker, to contain multitudinous contradictions, and yet, unlike that speaker, also self-evacuated, unable to assert an autonomous identity against those who would impose their own law upon it: "'He is capable of seeing the other side. He is a man who harbours contradictions.' I was ready to say to Guy, 'Here's a Marine recruit who reads Karl Marx.' I was ready to say, 'This boy is sitting on the scales, ready to be tilted either way'" (319).

DeLillo's Oswald is an inveterate role-player, but his adoption of various personas suggests, at last, a trivialized and sterile form of Odysseus's opportunistic performances or Whitman's expansive identifications. Where these precursors seem resolutely in control of their playacting, writing their own lines and preserving a sense of self distinct from the role, Oswald tends to lose himself within the dramas others have scripted. DeLillo's disgruntled CIA agent, Win Everett, enlists his associates in constructing the self that Oswald will eventually become: "He would script a gunman out of ordinary dog-eared paper, the contents of a wallet. Parmenter would contrive to get document blanks from the Records Branch. Mackey would find a model for the character Everett was in the process of creating. They wanted a name, a face, a bodily frame they might use to extend their fiction into the world" (50). Specific agents organizing the assassination, along with seductive cinematic narratives generated within the nomistic world, combine to establish the conditions of Oswald's culminating moment of transcendence. He becomes a "transparent eyeball" watching television alone, fusing with a thoroughly mediated "Nature" as he encounters sentient, and idiosyncratically legible, presences there. The experience amounts to an ironic iteration of Emerson and Thoreau's self-augmenting ecstasies, with *themis* emerging as a mysterious but now resolutely human "They," and a resentment-driven *daemon* soliciting, as in Poe's stories, some violent antisocial outburst:

> [He . . .] felt connected to the events on the screen. It was like secret
> instructions entering the network of signals and broadcast bands,
> the whole busy air of transmission. Marina was asleep. They were
> running a message through the night into his skin. . . . The streets
> were dark. The house was dark except for the flickering screen. An
> old scratchy film that carried his dreams. Perfection of rage, perfec-
> tion of control, the fantasy of night. . . . Lee felt he was in the mid-
> dle of his own movie. They were running this thing just for him.
> (370)

Whatever autonomous selfhood Oswald thinks he has claimed is composed of media clichés, his definitive role cast by others.

Wandering through the American *urbs naturae*, Oswald searches for
the potential scene of his (paradoxically private) *aristeia*. Branch invokes
Thoreau's most famous phrase—and suggests the distance between
Transcendentalist autonomy and the pathologies of hyperautonomy—in
summing up the assassin's significance: "After Oswald, men in America
are no longer required to lead lives of *quiet desperation*. You apply for a
credit card, buy a handgun, travel through cities, suburbs and shopping
malls, anonymous, anonymous, looking for a chance to take a shot at the
first puffy empty famous face, just to let people know there is someone
out there who reads the papers" (181; italics added). Thoreau's cabin at
Walden Pond becomes, in the assassin's efforts at self-affirming rebellion, the place for "men in small rooms" to plot terminal versions of John
Brown's raid on Harpers Ferry without reference to "higher laws."

Mailer's apprehension of the "white negro's" absorption into the
American *nomos*—epitomized in his description of Gary Gilmore's
contemplation of his appearance on the cover of *Time* magazine with a
cast of other luminaries—is augmented by DeLillo in his descriptions of
Oswald's dreams of celebrity. After the assassination, the accused killer
considers the way in which he has claimed a share of the president's
renown for himself, since "[the] figure of the gunman in the window was
inextricable from the victim and his history" (435). Oswald confirms his
own ironic self-rebegetting when his crime prompts the media to celebrate him:

> [He] heard his name on the radios and TVs. Lee Harvey Oswald.
> It sounded extremely strange. He didn't recognize himself in the
> full intonation of the name. The only time he used his middle name
> was to write it on a form that had a space for that purpose. No
> one called him by that name. Now it was everywhere. He heard it

coming from the walls. Reporters called it out. Lee Harvey Oswald, Lee Harvey Oswald. (416)

The scene can be thought of as an ironic replaying of Cooper's description of Bumppo after his initiation into killing—and baptism as "Hawkeye"—in *Deerslayer.* Oswald awakens into a new life after his violent action, though the vacancy of the self created thereby is, of course, part of the logic of hyperautonomy. After being shot himself, Oswald's final impression of himself, as a televised image, is of an ungrounded, ecstatic persona: "He is a stranger, in a mask, falling" (440). The eunomic framework in which Boone and Bumppo took life is replaced here by the infinite and amoral "Nature" of mass mediation, into which Oswald is miserably absorbed.

One of the central protagonists of *Underworld,* Nick Shay, tellingly invokes Oswald (and an infamous, reputedly forged picture of him) in an anxious declaration of independence from the legacy of Cold War paranoia: "I believed we could know what was happening to us. We were not excluded from our own lives. That is not my head on someone else's body in the photograph that's introduced as evidence. I didn't believe that nations play-act on a grand scale. I lived in the real" (*Underworld* 82). Nick is acutely aware of the imperiled status of postmeridial American selfhood, which perfects the nascent disembodiment described by McCarthy in its tendency to blur the distinction between actual bodies and their mediation. An early screening of the Zapruder film, the serendipitous amateur recording of Kennedy's death, initiates another of DeLillo's characters into a frightening sense of how human conspiracies manipulate both bodies and information: "And oh shit, oh god it came from the front, didn't it?" (*Underworld* 489). Sinister nomistic powers— redolent of the totalitarian networks in Mailer's *An American Dream,* but more secular and global—connect everything to everything: "[Nick's brother Matt] thought of the photograph of Nixon and wondered if the state had taken on the paranoia of the individual or was it the other way around. . . . And how can you tell the difference between orange juice and agent orange if the same massive system connects them at levels outside your comprehension?" (465).

Nick works for a large waste-disposal company and seems himself to epitomize the spiritual remainder or ideological slough of earlier forms of American autonomy. His last name contains an ironic allusion, perhaps, to Shays' Rebellion of 1786–87, an event which prompted Thomas

Jefferson's provocative defense of revolutionary violence: "What signify a few lives lost in a century or two? The tree of liberty must be refreshed from time to time with the blood of patriots and tyrants. It is it's [sic] natural manure" (Jefferson, "To William S. Smith" 911). In late capitalist America, Nick observes, corporate powers promise to obviate the need for rebellion by democratizing (at least some) access to technology and the sense it fosters of a liberating personal autonomy: "You feel the contact points around you, the caress of linked grids that give you a sense of order and command. It's there in the warbling banks of phones, in the fax machines and photocopiers and all the oceanic logic stored in your computer. Bemoan technology all you want. It expands your self-esteem and connects you in your well-pressed suit to the things that slip through the world otherwise unperceived" (89). Simultaneously, however, corporate culture forecloses on the self's potential for genuine rebellion: "Corporations are great and appalling things. They take you and shape you in nearly nothing flat, twist and swivel you. And they do it without overt persuasion, they do it with smiles and nods, a collective inflection of the voice. You stand at the head of a corridor and by the time you walk to the far end you have adopted the comprehensive philosophy of the firm, the *Weltanschauung*" (282). Reflecting on the "curious connection between weapons and waste," Nick articulates the essential logic of hyperautonomy, in which an extension of the liberty of the self to define and graze its own pasture ultimately and paradoxically dissolves that self into its *nomos*: "What we excrete comes back to consume us" (791).

Nick's firsthand participation in American violence occurred as a teenager when he accidentally killed a man with a shotgun. The outlaw or antinomian figure, and its associations with (as Mailer would term it) a "psychopathic" autonomy, remains attractive to him in middle age:

> I've always been a country of one. There's a certain distance in my makeup, a measured separation like my old man's, I guess, that I've worked at times to reduce, or thought of working, or said the hell with it.
>
> I like to tell my wife. I say to my wife. I tell her not to give up on me. I tell her there's an Italian word, or a Latin word, that explains everything. Then I tell her the word.
>
> She says, What does this explain? And she answers, Nothing.
>
> The word that explains nothing in this case is *lontananza*. Distance or remoteness, sure. But as I use the word, as I interpret it,

hard-edged and fine-grained, it's the perfected distance of the gangster, the syndicate mobster—the made man. Once you're a made man, *you don't need the constant living influence of sources outside yourself.* You're all there. You're made. You're handmade. You're a sturdy Roman wall. (275; italics added)

The Emerson we hear in these lines—"Ne te quaesiveris extra" (Do not seek yourself outside [yourself]) is the first epigraph of the essay "Self-Reliance" (132)—has been silted over by twentieth-century America's lurid rendering of outlaw mythology ("Underworld," as DeLillo surely knew, is itself the title of a 1927 gangster film). Like Jack in *White Noise* and Oswald in *Libra*, Nick depends upon cinematic clichés in his understanding of self-reliance as a separation—potentially if not actually violent—from nomistic bonds.

A genuine corporate man and no gangster, Nick's actual transgressions, save his teenage conviction for manslaughter, are only imaginary. The novel's authentic hyperautonomist is found in one of his dark doubles, Richard Henry Gilkey, a.k.a. The Texas Highway Killer. DeLillo introduces Gilkey in a chapter entitled "ELEGY FOR LEFT HAND ALONE, MID-1980s—EARLY 1990s" (153). Gilkey is the elegiac subject here, an urban frontiersman able to shoot accurately with his left hand while driving, his anachronistic gunslinger's skill unappreciated in contemporary America. Boone or Bumppo's skill at erotic "penetration" of the (feminine) wilderness is replaced here by a narcissistic self-containment, a masturbatory dead-end. Gilkey hunts his prey not, of course, in the wilderness, but on highways, that meretricious topography of postmeridial autonomy with its lone drivers in insulated cars (another of DeLillo's "small rooms"). His serial crimes suggest, more specifically, a travestied recapitulation of the exploits of William F. Cody, a.k.a. "Buffalo Bill," an actual frontiersman who starred in the melodrama "The Red Right Hand; or, The First Scalp for Custer" (Slotkin, *Gunfighter* 72) in the late nineteenth century. In his Wild West show, Cody sought to dramatize the frontier experience by staging quasi-historical events as public entertainment. The central scene in his performance involved a reenactment of his killing of Yellow Hand, a Cheyenne he encountered while travelling as a scout with the Fifth Cavalry. Slotkin notes the prominent theatricality of the incident even before its staging in the Wild West show—that is, the extent to which Cody's "natural" encounter with a hostile other was already implicated in its own commercial mediation. Cody put on highly stylized dress before heading into battle, choosing "the sort of costume that dime-novel illustrations had led the public to suppose was the proper dress of the wild Westerner" (Slotkin, *Gunfighter* 72). The frontiersman's *aristeia* becomes a self-conscious, proleptic "return" to primitivist vigor, dependent upon commercial clichés: "[Cody] was preparing for that moment when he would stand before his audience, wearing the figurative laurels of the day's battle and the vaquero suit, able to declare with truth that he stood before them in a plainsman's authentic garb, indeed the very clothes he had worn when he took 'The First Scalp for Custer'" (72).

A century after the Wild West shows, Gilkey updates Cody by starring, unwittingly and without any directorial control, in his own spectacular melodrama. One of his shootings is, like Oswald's assassination of Kennedy, accidentally recorded on amateur videotape, then endlessly broadcast on television. With the recasting of his act as commercially manipulated entertainment, command over his own act of rebellion, and any regenerative violence he might have wished for, are usurped by the depersonalizing *nomos* from which he had hoped to detach himself. As DeLillo's narrator suggests, there is something troublingly appropriate about the convergence of serial murder and serial mediation: "Taping-and-playing intensifies and compresses the event. It dangles a need to do it again. You sit there thinking that the serial murder has found its medium, or vice versa—an act of shadow technology, of compressed time and repeated images, stark and glary and unremarkable" (159). The repeated showings of Gilkey's videotaped crime on television reduce it to mere entertainment, while the murderer's own agency is usurped by the technology used to record it. Timothy L. Parrish explains the logic of equivalency functioning in this event: "In this context, the random shooter Gilkey is in turn 'shot' by the random camera holder. The camera does not record what he did, but changes the reality in which he acted. Likewise, allowing for the differences between film and video, we can see how the 'identity' of Gilkey or Oswald can be broken down, rewound, and cut up in the same way one splices a film. Technology creates a mass death wish that advertisers and Texas Highway Killers gratify even as we consume it" (Parrish 710). Gilkey's serial outrages are thus oddly in harmony with the American *nomos*: he acts in order to establish a sense of self-law and define his difference from his community as some kind of rugged *idiotes*, but his attempts only reconfirm his powerlessness and final anonymity within the dominant nomistic order. As Mark Seltzer describes such "primitivist" violence and its technocratic absorption, this is "the wild work of male repetitive violence

[. . . which] incorporates the life process and the machine process such that the call of the wild represents not the antidote to machine culture but its realization" (Seltzer 81). Regenerative violence becomes impossible here because the transgressive, ostensibly self-liberating act begets only its own duplication: murder demands further murder, and the self is not augmented but usurped in the mediated process. As Nick puts it, "Because once the tape starts rolling it can only end one way. This is what the context requires" (159–60).

Gilkey's ironic *aristeia* as a highway killer thus epitomizes the self-cancelling conditions of hyperautonomy. What Myra Jehlen traces as "American incarnation," a radical blending of the human with the natural world, reaches a baroque culmination in DeLillo's representation of the "undead" dissolution of the self into its *nomos*. The hyperautonomist represents a neutered version of what Emerson celebrates as a "possession" of the world, reversing the positive dimensions of the autonomous self who in "discovering his entire correspondence with nature writes himself universally large" (Jehlen 123). Autonomy functions for Emerson in terms of a centrifugal dynamic, a radiation of the magnified (essentially deified) self outward in its mastering containment of all that it beholds (and is) in Nature. The "truest and best creations" of that self have a secretarial quality, as Jehlen puts it, for they are essentially "dictations from nature" (96–97). DeLillo's Gilkey, in contrast, extends the logic of dictation to the point of that self's disappearance: here we discover a terminal version of the autonomous self, merely and sterilely passive as it "takes dictation" from a relentlessly mediated "Nature" now wholly claimed, and offered back to the self, by its *nomos*. The centrifugal dynamic of the Emersonian autonomist becomes definitively centripetal in the hyperautonomist, *into whose* blank receptivity the most general features of the nomistic world are projected.

What Seltzer calls "the mass in person"—a form of selfhood involving a sense of "direct *fusion* with an indistinct mass of others: the complete fusion with the mass at the expense of the individual" (Seltzer 19)—suggests the terms of Gilkey's collapsed autonomy. Like DeLillo's Oswald, who "looks like everybody" (*Libra* 300), the serial killer, argues Seltzer, "typifies typicality, the becoming abstract and general of the individuality of the individual" (Seltzer 34). What DeLillo's narrator calls in *Underworld* "a certain furtive sameness, a planing away of particulars" (786) that is the hallmark of late capitalism, finds its ultimate representative in this figure, who tends to adopt others' desire as his own (rather than, as Emerson had hoped, fulfilling a unique creative potential as he "writes himself universally large"). Gilkey lives in the third person, self-estranged in self-pasture, and the free indirect discourse DeLillo uses to characterize this unhappy and volatile "mass in person" is thus uncannily appropriate:

> He was not left-handed but taught himself to shoot with the left hand. This is what Bud would never understand, how he had to take his feelings outside himself so's to escape his isolation. He taught himself based on the theory that if you are driving with your right hand and sitting snug to the door it is better practically speaking to keep the right hand on the wheel and project the left hand out the window, the gun hand, so you do not have to fire across your body. He could probably talk to Bud about this and Bud might understand. But he would never understand how Richard had to take everything outside, share it with others, become part of the history of others, because this was the only way to escape, to get out from under the pissant details of who he was. (266)

Gilkey's deepest fear—understandably for such a figure—is of nonbeing: "When he first walked in the house and Bud barely noticed him, it was like the normalcy of dying. It was the empty hollow thing of not being here. A forty-mile drive into being transparent, awful but not unaccustomed" (268). This is transparency not as possibility—a mastering eyeball absorbing all—but as mere nothingness, a self-pasture amounting to a vacant self-inhabitance.

It is, as in DeLillo's other works, technological mediations which promise, and then nullify, vast self-augmentation. Calling in to a live television broadcast hosted by a woman with whom he is in love, Gilkey is teased with a brief validation: "She made him feel real, talking on the phone. She gave him the feeling he was taking shape as himself, coming into the shape he'd always been intended to take, the thing of who he really was" (269). In explaining his violence, he struggles to prove that his acts are meaningful and have been freely chosen: "Let's set the record straight. I did not grow up with head trauma. I had a healthy, basically, type childhood" (216). The irony and bathos here are heightened not just by Gilkey's reliance on verbal clichés—the idiom of the failed American *idiotes*, the "mass in person"—but by the use of a machine to disguise, and radically depersonalize, his voice: "The odd sound of the caller's voice, leveled-out, with faint tremors at the edges, odd little electronic storms, like someone trying to make a human utterance out of itemized data" (217). Instead of personal redemption, Gilkey achieves a kind of temporary media apotheosis: "He talked to her on the phone and made eye contact with the TV. This was the waking of the knowledge that he was real. This alien-eyed woman with raving hair sending emanations that astonished his heart. He spoke more confidently as time went on. He was coming into himself" (270). Appropriately, Gilkey is foiled by technocratic bureaucracy in his attempts at transcendence, rebuffed by an uncomprehending switchboard operator who will not let him speak for himself within the network of mediations which have temporarily established his individual prominence. His fantasy of a high-profile arrest confirms his self-effacing derivativeness and failure of agency as an outlaw, as it repeats the well-known details of another famous killer, Oswald, in custody at the Dallas Police Department: "He would have surrendered . . . in a blaze of lights, Richard Henry Gilkey, hustled down a hallway with Stetsoned men all around him and Sue Ann Corcoran by his side" (270).

Gilkey's attempt at articulating some kind of distinctive message is further undermined by the "taunting presence" of a copycat killer, who provokes the anxiety of the classic doppelgänger: "I know who I am. Who is he?" (272). Joel Black points out that the "relative banality of [copycat crimes] stems from the fact that what is being imitated in most of these cases is not the motive of the murderer or suicide victim, which is often unknown and unreported, but merely the external manner and circumstances of the death—in short, its *style*" (Black 10). Style (that is, nomistic convention) trumps individuality in such events, and the acts of both the original criminal and his imitator tend to be emptied of any significance beyond their own mediation: "Our post-transgressive age marks the fulfilment of McLuhan's dictum about the medium becoming the message . . . 'Meaning' at this juncture repeatedly reveals itself to be merely a function or fictional 'special effect' of the mass media" (137). Gilkey (along with his "message") is displaced by the determinations of mass technology, and at last he is simply forgotten. Uncaptured but radically consumed, he has amounted to little more than another disposable product: "No one talks about the Texas Highway Killer anymore. You never hear the name. The name used to be in the air, always on the verge of being spoken, of reentering the broadcast band and causing a brief excitation along the lined highways, but the shootings have evidently ended and the name is gone now" (807).

The autonomous self's undeath—the point of utter assimilation into, rather than detachment from, the nomistic operations of the commercial world—is echoed in Nick's remarks about a proposed advertising campaign at his former company that involved hiring a convicted terrorist to sell lawn products:

> George Metesky was the Mad Bomber of the 1940s and 1950s,
> famous for setting off a series of blasts at New York landmarks.
> They wanted to track him down at the state pen or the funny farm
> and build the whole campaign around his ancient and fabled deeds
> and his endorsement of the product.
> *Bomb your lawn with Nitrotex.* (528)

Another violent offender, the anonymous murderer of a homeless child named Esmeralda, is similarly absorbed into anonymous media replication, this time Internet reality, his act wholly impersonal and incommunicable: "After he does it, driving it in and spilling it out, he hits her one last time, hard, whore, and drags her up on the ledge and leans her over and lets her go. You dead, bitch. Then he goes back to thinking his nighttime thoughts. Screen reads *Searching*" (818).

The pointless destruction caused by Gilkey and related figures in *Underworld* suggests, finally, a revision of Slotkin's classic formula of American mythology in the hyperautonomist: not regeneration of the self through violence, but the regeneration of violence through repetition, by what is left of the self consumed in, and by, self-pasture.

Epilogue: Autonomy's Posthuman Dénouement

*The Staatling-Wapachung bigwigs were dressed like young kids, a lot
of vintage Zoo York Basic Cracker hoodies from the 2000s, and tons of
dechronification, making me think they were actually their own children.*
                    —SHTEYNGART, *SUPER SAD TRUE LOVE STORY*

American autonomy has always privileged *newness*, a reinvention and
augmentation of possibilities for the self and the nation in defiance of the
tyranny of the old. Jefferson, writing to James Madison from Paris in the
fall of 1789, has this to say about the priority of the living over the dead:

> The question Whether one generation of men has a right to bind
> another, seems never to have been started either on this or our side
> of the water. Yet it is a question of such consequences as not only
> to merit decision, but place also, among the fundamental prin-
> ciples of every government. The course of reflection in which we
> are immersed here on the elementary principles of society has
> presented this question to my mind; and that no such obligation
> can be transmitted I think very capable of proof. I set out on this
> ground which I suppose to be self-evident, *"that the earth belongs in
> usufruct to the living,"* that the dead have neither powers nor rights
> over it. ("To James Madison" [1789] 959)

Thoreau, in one of *Walden*'s most brazen passages, articulates a more
personal endorsement of youth:

> Old deeds for old people, and new deeds for new. Old people did
> not know enough once, perchance, to fetch fresh fuel to keep the
> fire a-going; new people put a little dry wood under a pot, and are
> whirled round the globe with the speed of birds, in a way to kill old
> people, as the phrase is. Age is no better, hardly so well, qualified

for an instructor as youth, for it has not profited so much as it has lost. One may almost doubt if the wisest man has learned anything of absolute value by living. (9)

Jefferson and Thoreau did not anticipate, of course, the advent of a mechanized autonomy that obviates distinctions between the living and the dead, and diffuses the self within an ahistorical present, where it may claim unlimited usufruct rights from Nature's God. Under such conditions, the commitment to liberating each generation from its ancestors, and insisting on the importance of derogating historical authority in order to cultivate the freshness and receptivity of youth, might itself become tyrannical.

Gary Shteyngart's satirical novel *Super Sad True Love Story* (2010; hereafter *SSTLS*) vividly illustrates that tyranny as it explores some twenty-first-century permutations of autonomy's undeath. Here, rather than the emerging phenomenon it is in DeLillo, hyperautonomy is a well-established, even banal fact of contemporary eunomic dissolution. The bodiless liberation prophesied in McCarthy's meridial horsemen—whose shadows flit "like shapes capable of violating their covenant with the flesh that authored them and continuing autonomous across the naked rock without reference to sun or man or god" (McCarthy 139)—seems to have entered a sort of democratized dénouement within horizonless virtual worlds. The nascent Internet represented in *Underworld*, still a curiosity to most Americans, has metastasized into a totalizing episteme, and become the hyperautonomist's primary, posthuman pasture. So advanced is contemporary technological mastery in Shteyngart's near-future America, moreover, that the previously intransigent and perishable "not me" of the flesh itself has been almost completely assimilated into the ambit of the human will. Having largely annexed Jefferson's originary Laws of Nature and Nature's God, contemporary Americans can now plausibly assume—in a hubristic leap unimaginable to the ancient Greeks—that they will soon have the means to nullify aging and natural death, and thus overcome, in a strangely self-annihilating process of self-deification, the last barrier separating them from the divine. "NATURE," according to the slogan of one of the book's ominous global corporations, "HAS A LOT TO LEARN FROM US" (60).

America itself disintegrates as a political entity, in Shteyngart's imagining, after having emptied its originary commitment to personal autonomy of its positive, productive potential. The novel's presiding villain, the weirdly "de-chronified" septuagenarian Joshua "Joshie" Goldman, sums up the transition to America's next iteration in a climactic speech to his corporate employees. All means are justified, he argues, in attempting to preserve whatever remains of American greatness: "Because we are the last, best hope for this nation's future" (181). Joshie reworks, of course, the conclusion to Lincoln's address to Congress in 1862: "In giving freedom to the slave we assure freedom to the free—honourable alike in what we give and what we preserve. We shall nobly save or meanly lose the last best hope of earth" (Lincoln 639). Lincoln himself was reworking Jefferson—who lauded "this Government, the world's best hope" ("First Inaugural" 493)—in his first inaugural address. Significantly, however, Joshie's "we" substitutes himself and his corporation's interests in place of republican government; for him, the "last, best hope" of the entire world is a thoroughly commercial *nomos*, providing a technologically empowered autonomy to an elite who may claim *themis* as their own. Any violent action is justified in defense of that "hope," Joshie implies, for the tree of liberty must be refreshed, once again, with the blood of those who would resist its newest germination.

SSTLS gives us an American citizenry anxious about national decline, but largely distracted by a dazzling range of consumer choices and means to celebrate the self. Most of these are made available through a sort of super-smartphone called an "äppärät," which offers a cosmic fecundity of identifications that would have overwhelmed even Whitman. The Transcendentalists' emphasis on personal renovation—what Bloom characterized as the "last Western Sublime," an utter emancipation from tradition in an act of self-rebegetting (*Poetry* 244)—reemerges here as a trivializing commitment to "youthfulness," vulgarly irreverent toward the authority of the past and fixated on callow gratifications. Shteyngart's desperate and unquiet hyperautonomists seem, in fact, like late-stage elaborations of the mid-nineteenth-century conformists condemned by Thoreau, those who have "no time to be any thing but a machine" and have become "the tools of their tools" (Thoreau, *Walden* 7, 32). Though coyly deployed without explanation, the word "apparat" itself—its English sense, "the party machine of the Communist party in Russia," derives from the Latin *apparātus*, "instrument" (*OED*)—implies the precise logic of hyperautonomy. Those who use the device (and who are, in fact, literally *leashed* to it) are ironically subject to totalitarian control, losing themselves within various corporate manipulations and the meretricious attractions of youth culture's exhibitionism and materialism, even as they seek, and consider themselves to be indulging, a fluid range of virtual personae.

DeLillo's representations of hyperautonomous selves who have been dissolved into the technological means of their own celebration—Oswald's discovery of himself onscreen, the Texas Highway Killer's absorption into video loops—suggest a kind of wide-eyed recognition of something novel and forbidding in the American imaginary. In Shteyngart, the phenomenon is rendered as part of the banal (synthetic) fabric of the everyday: personal identity is intimately woven into virtual networks, which are used to apprehend the reality of other selves and to compose a provisional "song of myself" (instantly and interminably updateable, in a way that Whitman surely would have envied). *Not* to be on these networks, as a manipulable identity endlessly evolving out of torrents of shared data, is *not to be*. Superficially contemptuous of social bonds and aggressively self-promoting—the undead residua of the Transcendentalists' deification of the self—the hyperautonomist is, nevertheless, hardly distinguishable from the corporate machinations of his *nomos* (suggesting, once again, how inadequate "individual" is for these contemporary selves who are not at all divided from larger wholes). Commercial and political interests construct the cybernetic pastures where hyperautonomists graze, monitoring and shaping where and how that grazing takes place. The detachment necessary to the life of the *idiotes*, a distance from social conventions and coercions, has become essentially unthinkable.

Lenny Abramov, the thirty-nine-old-year-old protagonist of *SSTLS*, resists some of the attractions of American youth culture, and is something of a throwback to earlier stages of the nation's cultural history (he would prefer to *read*, for instance, rather than "scan text"), yet he remains profoundly implicated in this brave new world of democratized and technologized self-pasture. A salesman in the "Post-Human Services division" (5) of a powerful corporation, he sells "dechronification treatments" (63) that promise eternal life. He begins the novel by declaring that he has decided he will himself never die: "I will need to re-grow my melting liver, replace the entire circulatory system with 'smart blood,' and find someplace safe and warm (but not too warm) to while away the angry seasons and the holocausts. And when the earth expires, as it surely must, I will leave it for a new earth, greener still but with fewer allergens" (5). In a scene emphasizing the superficiality and crudity of contemporary social relations, along with the transparency and vulnerability of the self constructed within them, Lenny visits a nightclub and is encouraged by his friends to use his äppärät to "form a community," or "FAC" (88), with a group of strangers. The enchiridion of his self—age, address, income, health status, consumer history, credit score, psychological profile, sexual preferences—is instantly shared (some of the data has been submitted voluntarily, some of it generated automatically). The "community" thus formed is exceptionally porous, mutable, ephemeral, its members furiously manipulating, and manipulated by, their own celebration. Lenny rates others in the bar on their attractiveness, and in turn is rated by them: "Streams of data were now fighting for time and space around us. The pretty girl I had just FACed was projecting my MALE HOTNESS as 120 out of 800, PERSONALITY 450, and something called SUSTAINABILIT¥ at 630. The other girls were sending me similar figures" (90–91). The comic humiliation here, as Lenny angles for and provisionally nets a self within the "streams of data" engineered by corporate powers, underscores the mundane self-negations of hyperautonomy in the age of social networking.

The äppäräti used by Shteyngart's hyperautonomists allow them to range across a much wider consumer pasture, and a much more thoroughly virtualized one, than that sketched by DeLillo. They commune with and command what is left of *themis* while scoping, as fevered and "instrumentalized" transparent eyeballs, limitless commercial prospects. Lenny describes a characteristically trivial moment of *aristeia* within contemporary America's sacred hunting grounds as he observes his much younger girlfriend, Eunice Park (*eu-nike* as "good victory" in the contemporary *urbs naturae*), shop for clothes: "Here was the anxiety of choice, the pain of living without history, the pain of some higher need. I felt humbled by this world, awed by its religiosity, the attempt to extract meaning from an artifact that contained mostly thread" (208–9). The divine is, Shteyngart implies, as comprehensively synthetic as the clothes Lenny and Eunice pursue ("Composition—7 percent elastane, 2 percent polyester . . . 50 percent rayon viscose" [210]), a complex and routine construction of some collective human agency.[1] The clothed self—what Thoreau contemptuously called "our outmost cuticle and mortal coil" (Thoreau, *Walden* 21)—eclipses any significant inward counterpart. To shop is to find oneself—in a direct inversion of Emerson's motto from "Self-Reliance," *Ne te quaesiveris extra*—outside (oneself), as one assumes a variety of commercially mediated, crassly eroticized personae: "Here were the famous nippleless Saaami bras that Eunice had shown me on AssLuxury and the fabled Padma corsets that the Polish porn star wore on AssDoctor. We stopped to look at some conservative Juicy-Pussy summer cocktail dresses" (208). Though Eunice feels an inchoate attraction to her parents' Christianity (itself debased by commercialism in Shteyngart's satire) and retains compassionate instincts, her deep private self—what Emerson would have advised her to *trust*—barely exists beneath her role as a networked consumer.

Given the broad contours of these concluding stages of the story I have been telling, what might be said about the "negative space" on the other side of this essentially literary border?

In problematizing the constitutive elements of auto-nomy ("self"-"pasture/rule"), the media age has radically problematized the concept of autonomy itself. What sense can we make of "self-rule" when the self is deliquescing into virtual, selfless selves, and the rules of its expression are being fundamentally rewritten? When the whole notion of "rule" is itself being radically revised? What sense can we make of self-pasture when not merely is the Nature in which it is grounded being de-natured, but even the most useful and accessible metaphorical senses of "pasture" are being reconfigured in the disembodied, decentralized space of digitized memory and experience?

And from this profound and now problematized conceptual nexus of autonomy stretch a whole series of now problematized conceptual vectors, extending deeply into contemporary sociopolitical debate. Problems of identity, of property and the proprietary, of the nature and structure of authority and authenticity (both rooted in the "auto" of autonomy), of radically new and unstable relationships between traditionally themistic and nomistic elements in society and the self; and equally fundamental and pressing—especially for a people that has from its inception defined itself in a hermeneutic dialectic with its environment—problems of the self's relation to its ancestral pasture, its natural environment, which now, in a seemingly very dangerous and unstable inversion, "has a lot to learn from us"; all these intersect and interact in the nexus of autonomy.

Exploring such topics must be the work of other, very different studies, but this much seems clear from the present one: there will be no therapeutic cure for the concept of autonomy in the American imaginary. Either its original eunomic roots are (perhaps painfully) reasserted in some new (but very old) form, as in the Native Americans' circle of life, for example, or the concept, as traditionally understood, appears likely to become a kind of dead star, with enormous and enduring gravity, but little light, or heat, or life.

Notes

Introduction

1. All translations are mine unless otherwise indicated.

2. See, in particular, Caroline Winterer's *The Culture of Classicism: Ancient Greece and Rome in American Intellectual Life, 1780–1910* (Johns Hopkins UP, 2004); Carl J. Richard's *The Founders and the Classics: Greece, Rome, and the American Enlightenment* (Harvard UP, 1994) and *The Golden Age of the Classics: Greece, Rome, and the Antebellum United States* (Harvard UP, 2009); and Meyer Reinhold's *Classica Americana: The Greek and Roman Heritage in the United States* (Wayne State UP, 1984).

3. All definitions have been adapted from Liddell and Scott's *English/Greek Lexicon*.

4. The story I tell here is, I suggest, fundamental to the history of America, and these are but two of the most important (but far from the only interesting) areas of study related to it. Comparisons of this narrative to the similar but importantly different literary histories of other English-speaking nations—or, say, of the West generally, or of Middle Eastern and Eastern cultures, where the dream and pursuit of personal autonomy is far less important—also seem worthy of their own independent and extensive treatment.

5. The novel's full title is *Wieland: or, The Transformation: An American Tale.*

Chapter 2

1. Jefferson's conception of those rights now seems, of course, repellently compromised in its restriction of full liberty to white men. A slaveholder until the end of his life, Jefferson cites in *Notes on the State of Virginia* (1781) the "real distinctions which nature has made" (*Notes* 264) between blacks and whites, while derogating Native Americans as primitives.

Chapter 4

1. The five authors covered in this chapter evolved profoundly over time, of course, and it would be (at best) misleading to suggest that their extensive bodies of work are internally consistent and without contradiction (they are large, and contain

multitudes). However, since my aim here is to illustrate a specific stage in the growth of personal autonomy, I have, for the sake of convenience, focused on well-known and influential works, each of which I take to be broadly representative of the authors' conception of American self-pasture.

2. The essay was first published under the title "Resistance to Civil Government."

3. See, in particular, "The Cask of Amontillado," "The Tell-tale Heart," "The Black Cat," "The Pit and the Pendulum," "The Fall of the House of Usher," and "The Premature Burial."

4. Poe's quotation condenses part of the actual Homeric lines: "The mist, moreover, have I taken from your eyes that formerly was upon them, so that now you may perceive both god and man" (*Iliad* 5.127–28).

Chapter 6

1. See also Neil Campbell: "McCarthy's *Blood Meridian* is the point at which one reaches the climax of life and simultaneously recognizes the proximity, even the inevitability of its end. The blood is both life-giving and life-destroying, hence the qualification of the novel's title by 'or the evening redness in the west', reminding us of a larger mythic fear about the West as a place where even the sun dies" (Campbell 221). For an excellent discussion of the relevance to the novel of "meridian" as a geographical dividing line, and as a historical division between an anarchic or "antinomian" past and "our more subtle moral order" (Ellis 94), see Jay Ellis's "'What Happens to Country' in *Blood Meridian*," *Rocky Mountain Review of Language and Literature* 60.1 (2006): 85–97.

Epilogue

1. From the Greek verb *tithenai*, "to put in place," come both the adjective *synthetikos*, "to put in place together," and the name of the goddess *Themis*, "she who puts [law/custom/convention] in place."

Works Cited

Anderson, Quentin. *The Imperial Self: An Essay in American Literary and Cultural History.* New York: Knopf, 1971.

Baudrillard, Jean. "Consumer Society." *Selected Writings of Jean Baudrillard.* Edited by Mark Poster. Stanford UP, 1988.

Bellah, Robert N., et al. *Habits of the Heart: Individualism and Commitment in American Life.* Berkeley: U of California P, 2008.

Berlin, Isaiah. "The Birth of Greek Individualism: A Turning Point in the History of Political Thought." *Liberty.* Edited by Henry Hardy. Oxford: Oxford UP, 2008.

Black, Joel. *The Aesthetics of Murder: A Study in Romantic Literature and Contemporary Culture.* Baltimore: John Hopkins UP, 1991.

Bloom, Harold. *The American Religion: The Emergence of the Post-Christian Nation.* New York: Simon and Schuster, 1992.

———. *How to Read and Why.* New York: Scribner, 2000.

———. *Poetry and Repression.* New Haven: Yale UP, 1976.

Braswell, William. "Melville as a Critic of Emerson." *American Literature* 9.3 (Nov. 1937): 317–34.

Brown, Charles Brockden. "Letter to Thomas Jefferson, December 15, 1798." *Wieland and Memoirs of Carwin the Biloquist.* Edited by Bryan Waterman. New York: Norton, 2011.

———. *Wieland and Memoirs of Carwin the Biloquist.* Edited by Bryan Waterman. New York: Norton, 2011.

Brown, Meredith Mason. *Frontiersman: Daniel Boone and the Making of America.* Baton Rouge: Louisiana State UP, 2008.

Buell, Lawrence. *Emerson.* Cambridge: Harvard UP, 2003.

Byron, Lord. "Don Juan." *Byron: Poetical Works*. Edited by Frederick Page. Oxford: Oxford UP, 1970.

Campbell, Neil. "Liberty Beyond Its Proper Bounds: Cormac McCarthy's History of the West in *Blood Meridian*." *Myth, Legend, Dust: Critical Responses to Cormac McCarthy*. Edited by Rick Wallach. Manchester: Manchester UP, 2000.

Cavell, Stanley. *The Senses of Walden*. Chicago: U of Chicago P, 1992.

Cooper, James Fenimore. *The Deerslayer*. New York: Viking Penguin, 1987.

———. *The Last of the Mohicans*. New York: Penguin, 1982.

———. *The Pioneers*. New York: Signet Classics, 1964.

Crèvecoeur, J. Hector St. John de. *Letters from an American Farmer*. Oxford: Oxford UP, 1997.

DeCurtis, Anthony. "Interview with Don DeLillo." *Introducing Don DeLillo*. Edited by Frank Lentricchia. Durham: Duke UP, 1999.

DeLillo, Don. "The American Absurd." *Harper's* Feb. 2004: 32.

———. *Americana*. Boston: Houghton Mifflin, 1971.

———. *Libra*. New York: Penguin, 1989.

———. *Underworld*. New York: Scribner, 1997.

———. *White Noise*. New York: Penguin, 1985.

Douglass, Wayne J. "The Criminal Psychopath as Hollywood Hero." *Journal of Popular Film and Television* 8.4 (Winter 1981): 30–39.

Eagleton, Terry. *Holy Terror*. Oxford: Oxford UP, 2005.

Ellis, Bret Easton. *American Psycho*. New York: Vintage, 1991.

Ellis, Jay. "'What Happens to Country' in *Blood Meridian*." *Rocky Mountain Review of Language and Literature* 60.1 (2006): 85–97.

Emerson, Ralph Waldo. "The American Scholar." *The Essential Writings of Ralph Waldo Emerson*. New York: Modern Library, 2000.

———. *The Journals and Miscellaneous Notebooks of Ralph Waldo Emerson*. Vols. 3, 5, and 7. Edited by William H. Gilman et al. Cambridge: Harvard UP, 1963–69.

———. *Nature*. *The Essential Writings of Ralph Waldo Emerson*. New York: Modern Library, 2000.

———. "The Over-Soul." *The Essential Writings of Ralph Waldo Emerson*. New York: Modern Library, 2000.

———. "Plato, or the Philosopher, from *Representative Men*." *The Essential Writings of Ralph Waldo Emerson*. New York: Modern Library, 2000.

———. "Poet." *The Essential Writings of Ralph Waldo Emerson*. New York: Modern Library, 2000.

———. "Self-Reliance." *The Essential Writings of Ralph Waldo Emerson*. New York: Modern Library, 2000.

———. *Two Unpublished Essays: The Character of Socrates, The Present State of Ethical Philosophy*. Boston: Lamson, Wolffe, & Co., 1895.

Engles, Tim. "'Who Are You, Literally?': Fantasies of the White Self in *White Noise*." *Modern Fiction Studies* 45.3 (1999): 755–87.

Filson, John. *The Discovery, Settlement and Present State of Kentucke.* 1784. Westminster: Heritage, 2007.

Flint, Timothy. *The Life and Adventures of Daniel Boone, the First Settler of Kentucky.* Cincinnati: U. P. James, 1868. Reprint of *Biographical Memoir of Daniel Boone, the First Settler of Kentucky.* 1833.

———. *Recollections of the last ten years, passed in occasional residences and journeyings in the valley of the Mississippi, from Pittsburg and the . . .* Boston: Cummings, Hilliard, and Company, 1826.

Hayes, Kevin J. *The Road to Monticello: The Life and Mind of Thomas Jefferson.* Oxford: Oxford UP, 2008.

Hemingway, Ernest. "The Battler." *The Complete Short Stories of Ernest Hemingway: The Finca Vigía Edition.* New York: Macmillan, 1987.

———. "Big Two-Hearted River." *The Complete Short Stories of Ernest Hemingway: The Finca Vigía Edition.* New York: Macmillan, 1987.

———. "Chapter VI." *The Complete Short Stories of Ernest Hemingway: The Finca Vigía Edition.* New York: Macmillan, 1987.

———. *The Complete Short Stories of Ernest Hemingway: The Finca Vigía Edition.* New York: Macmillan, 1987.

———. *A Farewell to Arms.* New York: Charles Scribner's Sons, 1957.

———. *The Green Hills of Africa.* New York: Scribner, 1998.

———. "Indian Camp." *The Complete Short Stories of Ernest Hemingway: The Finca Vigía Edition.* New York: Macmillan, 1987.

———. *The Sun Also Rises.* New York: Charles Scribner's Sons, 1970.

Hesiod. *Works and Days. The Perseus Project.* Edited by Gregory R. Crane. Mar. 1997. Dept. of Classics, Tufts U. 4 June 2010. www.perseus. tufts.edu/hopper/text?doc=Hes.+WD+274&fromdoc=Perseus%3Atext %3A1999.01.0131.

Homer. *The Iliad. The Perseus Project.* Edited by Gregory R. Crane. Mar. 1997. Dept. of Classics, Tufts U. 25 June 2010. www.perseus.tufts.edu/hopper/text? doc=Hom.+Il.+2.102&fromdoc=Perseus%3Atext%3A1999.01.0133.

———. *Odyssey. The Perseus Project.* Edited by Gregory R. Crane. Mar. 1997. Dept. of Classics, Tufts U. 5 Sept. 2010. www.perseus.tufts.edu/hopper/text?d oc=Hom.+Od.+16.400&fromdoc=Perseus%3Atext%3A1999.01.0135.

Hume, Kathryn. *American Dream, American Nightmare: American Fiction since 1960.* Urbana: U of Illinois P, 2002.

Jefferson, Thomas. "Crèvecoeur." *Thomas Jefferson: Writings.* New York: Library of America, 1984.

———. "Declaration of Independence." *Thomas Jefferson: Writings.* New York: Library of America, 1984.

———. "First Inaugural." *Thomas Jefferson: Writings.* New York: Library of America, 1984.

———. "Jefferson's Letter to the Danbury Baptists." Lib. of Cong. June 1998. 2 Nov. 2011. www.loc.gov/loc/lcib/9806/danpost.html.

———. *Notes on the State of Virginia. Thomas Jefferson: Writings.* New York: Library of America, 1984.

———. "A Summary View of the Rights of British America." *Thomas Jefferson: Writings.* New York: Library of America, 1984.

———. "To Charles Thomson." *Thomas Jefferson: Writings.* New York: Library of America, 1984

———. "To Henry Lee." *Thomas Jefferson: Writings.* New York: Library of America, 1984. 1500–1501.

———. "To James Madison. Paris, Dec. 20, 1787." *Thomas Jefferson: Writings.* New York: Library of America, 1984. 914–18.

———. "To James Madison. Paris, Sept. 6, 1789." *Thomas Jefferson: Writings.* New York: Library of America, 1984. 959–64.

———. "To John Adams. Monticello, Aug. 15, 1820." *Thomas Jefferson: Writings.* New York: Library of America, 1984.

———. "To Peter Carr.". *Thomas Jefferson: Writings.* New York: Library of America, 1984. 900–906

———. "To William Short." *Thomas Jefferson: Writings.* New York: Library of America, 1984. 1003–6.

———. "To William Short, with a Syllabus." *Thomas Jefferson: Writings.* New York: Library of America, 1984.

———. "To William S. Smith." *Thomas Jefferson: Writings.* New York: Library of America, 1984. 910–12.

Jehlen, Myra. *American Incarnation: The Individual, the Nation, and the Continent.* Cambridge: Harvard UP, 1986.

Keesey, Douglas. *Don DeLillo.* New York: Twayne, 1993.

Lawler, Peter Augustine. "Classical Ethics, Jefferson's Christian Epicureanism, and American Morality." *Perspectives on Political Science* 20.1 (Winter 1991): 17– 22.

Lawrence, D. H. *Studies in Classic American Literature.* London: Penguin, 1991.

Lewis, R. W. B. *The American Adam: Innocence, Tragedy, and Tradition in the Nineteenth Century.* Chicago: U of Chicago P, 1955.

Liddell, Henry George, and Robert Scott. *A Greek-English Lexicon. The Perseus Project.* Edited by Gregory R. Crane. Mar. 1997. Dept. of Classics, Tufts U. 5 Feb. 2010. www.perseus.tufts.edu/hopper/text?doc=Perseus%3Atext%3A199 9.04.0057%3Aentry%3Dau)to%2Fnomos.

Lincoln, Abraham. *Abraham Lincoln: His Speeches and Writings.* Edited by Roy Prentice Basler. Cleveland: Da Capo Press, 2001.

Lindberg, Gary. *The Confidence Man in American Literature.* New York: Oxford UP, 1982.

Mailer, Norman. *Advertisements for Myself.* New York: Berkley, 1959.

———. *An American Dream.* New York: Dell, 1965.

———. *The Executioner's Song.* Boston: Little, Brown, 1979.

——. *The Naked and the Dead.* New York: Holt, Rinehart, and Winston, 1948.

——. "The Ninth Presidential Paper: Totalitarianism." *The Presidential Papers.* New York: G. P. Putnam's Sons, 1963.

——. "Superman Comes to the Supermarket." *The Presidential Papers.* New York: G. P. Putnam's Sons, 1963.

——. "The White Negro: Superficial Reflections on the Hipster." *Advertisements for Myself.* New York: Berkley, 1959.

Marx, Leo. *The Machine in the Garden: Technology and the Pastoral Ideal in America.* 1964. Oxford: Oxford UP, 2000.

McCann, Sean. "The Imperiled Republic: Norman Mailer and the Poetics of Anti-Liberalism." *ELH* 67.1 (2000): 293–336.

McCarthy, Cormac. *Blood Meridian, Or The Evening Redness in the West.* New York: Vintage, 1992.

McClung, John A. *Sketches of Western Adventure: Containing an Account of the Most Interesting Incidents Connected with the Settlement of the West, from 1755 to 1794.* Covington: Richard H. Collins & Co., 1872.

Melville, Herman. *Moby Dick, or The Whale.* New York: Penguin, 1992.

Middlekauff, Robert. *The Glorious Cause: The American Revolution, 1763–1789.* Oxford: Oxford UP, 2005.

Miller, Charles A. *Jefferson and Nature: An Interpretation.* Baltimore: Johns Hopkins UP, 1988.

Muñoz, Vincent Phillip. *God and the Founders: Madison, Washington, Jefferson.* Cambridge: Cambridge UP, 2009.

Nietzsche, Friedrich. *Daybreak: Thoughts on the Prejudices of Morality.* Translated by R. J. Hollingdale. Cambridge: Cambridge UP, 1982.

——. *On the Genealogy of Morals. Ecce Homo.* Edited by Walter Kaufmann. Toronto: Vintage, 1969.

——. *Thus Spake Zarathustra: A Book for Everyone and Nobody.* Translated by Graham Parkes. Oxford: Oxford UP, 2005.

O'Brien, Conor Cruise. *The Long Affair: Thomas Jefferson and the French Revolution.* Chicago: U of Chicago P, 1996.

Ostwalt, Martin. *Nomos and the Beginnings of the Athenian Democracy.* Oxford: Clarendon Press, 1969.

Parrish, Timothy L. "From Hoover's FBI to Eisenstein's *Unterwelt*: DeLillo Directs the Postmodern Novel." *Modern Fiction Studies* 45.3 (1999): 696–723.

Patell, Cyrus R. K. *Negative Liberties: Morrison, Pynchon, and the Problem of Liberal Ideology.* Durham: Duke UP, 2001.

Plato. *Apology. The Perseus Project.* Edited by Gregory R. Crane. Mar. 1997. Dept. of Classics, Tufts U. 5 Nov. 2010. www.perseus.tufts.edu/hopper/text?doc=Plat.+Apol.+32a&fromdoc=Perseus%3Atext%3A1999.01.0169.

——. *Gorgias. The Perseus Project.* Edited by Gregory R. Crane. Mar. 1997. Dept. of Classics, Tufts U. 5 Nov. 2010. www.perseus.tufts.edu/hopper/text?doc=Plat.+Gorg.+483b&fromdoc=Perseus%3Atext%3A1999.01.0177.

Poe, Edgar Allan. "The Black Cat." *The Selected Writings of Edgar Allan Poe*. Edited by G. R. Thompson. New York: Norton, 2004.

———. "The Man of the Crowd." *The Selected Writings of Edgar Allan Poe*. Edited by G. R. Thompson. New York: Norton, 2004.

———. "William Wilson." *The Selected Writings of Edgar Allan Poe*. Edited by G. R. Thompson. New York: Norton, 2004.

Postman, Neil. *Amusing Ourselves to Death*. New York: Penguin, 1985.

Rahv, Philip. "Crime Without Punishment." Rev. of *An American Dream*, by Norman Mailer. *New York Review of Books* 25 March 1965: 1–4.

Rakove, Jack N., ed. *The Annotated U.S. Constitution and Declaration of Independence*. Cambridge: Harvard UP, 2009.

Richard, Carl J. *The Founders and the Classics*. Cambridge: Harvard UP, 1994.

Rogin, Michael Paul. *Fathers and Children: Andrew Jackson and the Subjugation of the American Indian*. New York: Vintage, 1975.

Roosevelt, Theodore. *The Strenuous Life*. New York: Review of Reviews, 1910.

Samuels, Shirley. "Patriarchal Violence, Federalist Panic, and *Wieland*." *Wieland and Memoirs of Carwin the Biloquist*. Edited by Bryan Waterman. New York: Norton, 2011. 393–406.

Sellers, Charles. *The Market Revolution: Jacksonian America, 1815–1846*. New York: Oxford UP, 1991.

Seltzer, Mark. *Serial Killers: Death and Life in America's Wound Culture*. New York: Routledge, 1998.

Sepich, John. *Notes on "Blood Meridian": Revised and Expanded Edition*. Austin: U of Texas P, 2008.

Shteyngart, Gary. *Super Sad True Love Story*. New York: Random House, 2010.

Slotkin, Richard. *Gunfighter Nation: The Myth of the Frontier in Twentieth-Century America*. Norman: U of Oklahoma P, 1998.

———. *Regeneration through Violence: The Mythology of the American Frontier, 1600–1860*. Norman: U of Oklahoma P, 1973.

Sophocles. *Antigone. The Perseus Project*. Edited by Gregory R. Crane. Mar. 1997. Dept. of Classics, Tufts U. 7 Mar. 2011. www.perseus.tufts.edu/hopper/text?doc=Soph.+Ant.+450&fromdoc=Perseus%3Atext%3A1999.01.0185.

Tanner, Tony. *The American Mystery*. Cambridge: Cambridge UP, 2000.

Thoreau, Henry David. "Civil Disobedience." *Walden, The Maine Woods, Collected Essays and Poems*. Edited by Robert F. Sayre and Elizabeth Hall Witherall. New York: Library of America, 2007.

———. "A Plea for Captain John Brown." *Walden, The Maine Woods, Collected Essays and Poems*. Edited by Robert F. Sayre and Elizabeth Hall Witherall. New York: Library of America, 2007.

———. "Slavery in Massachusetts." *Walden, The Maine Woods, Collected Essays and Poems*. Edited by Robert F. Sayre and Elizabeth Hall Witherall. New York: Library of America, 2007.

———. *Walden, or Life in the Woods. Walden, The Maine Woods, Collected*

Essays and Poems. Edited by Robert F. Sayre and Elizabeth Hall Witherall. New York: Library of America, 2007.

———. "Walking." *Walden, The Maine Woods, Collected Essays and Poems.* Edited by Robert F. Sayre and Elizabeth Hall Witherall. New York: Library of America, 2007.

———. "A Week on the Concord and Merrimack Rivers." *A Week on the Concord and Merrimack Rivers; Walden, Or, Life in the Woods; The Maine Woods; Cape Cod.* Edited by Robert F. Sayre. New York: Library of America, 1985.

———. *The Writings of Henry David Thoreau.* Vol. 6. New York: Houghton Mifflin, 1906. 295–96.

Tocqueville, Alexis de. *Democracy in America.* Vols. 1 & 2. Translated by Henry Reeves. New York: Bantam, 2004.

Twain, Mark. *Adventures of Huckleberry Finn.* Edited by Stephen Railton. Peterborough: Broadview, 2011.

Warren, Robert Penn. "Ernest Hemingway." *Modern Critical Views: Ernest Hemingway.* Edited by Harold Bloom. New York: Chelsea House, 1985.

Warshow, Robert. "The Gangster as Tragic Hero." *The Immediate Experience: Movies, Comics, Theatre & Other Aspects of Popular Culture.* New York: Doubleday, 1962.

Wenke, Joseph. *Mailer's America.* Hanover: UP of New England, 1987.

Wesley, Marilyn C. *Violent Adventure: Contemporary Fiction by Men.* Charlottesville: U of Virginia P, 2003.

Whitman, Walt. *The Complete Poems.* London: Penguin, 1986.

Wood, Gordon S. *Empire of Liberty: A History of the Early Republic, 1789–1815.* Oxford: Oxford UP, 2009.

Index

Cummings, General, 87, 88, 94, 100, 113

daemon, 25, 40, 54, 55, 61, 71, 86, 123
Declaration of Independence. *See* Thomas
Jefferson
DeLillo, Don, 5, 6, 15, 26, 33, 35, 48, 53, 58,
67, 70, 71, 75, 77, 97, 99, 112–32, 134,
136, 137
democracy, 20, 21, 52, 55, 58, 59, 60, 66, 69,
71, 74, 88, 99, 101, 105, 126, 134, 136;
Tocqueville's *Democracy in America*,
7, 76, 112
Diomedes, 72
Dionysus, 66
Douglass, Wayne J., 90
Dysnomia/*dysnomia*, 2, 113

Eagleton, Terry, 42
elenchus, 12, 14, 24, 26, 62, 74
Ellis, Bret Easton, 117
Ellis, Jay, 140n1 (chap. 6)
Emerson, Ralph Waldo, 3, 14, 26, 31, 38,
52, 55–61, 64, 68, 69, 72, 74, 76, 79, 86,
90, 92, 93, 98–99, 107, 111, 116, 123, 127,
129, 137, 138; *idiotes* and, 30, 54, 59–60,
122; *Nature*, 36, 56–58, 73, 101–3,
105, 106, 108, 122; "Self-Reliance,"
vii, 58–60, 90, 127, 137; "transparent
eyeball," 36, 57, 62, 63, 66, 101, 102, 113,
123, 130, 137
Engles, Tim, 115
Epicurus/Epicureanism, 12, 14, 17, 25–26,
28, 30–31, 41, 63, 64, 76, 78, 81–83, 113,
114, 119
Erdrich, Louise, 11
Eunomia/*eunomia*, 2, 4, 6, 7, 9, 12, 13, 27–
41, 43, 47, 50, 56, 64, 77, 138; eunomic
dissolution, 12, 14, 15, 22, 26, 44, 52, 53,
54, 66, 70, 74, 76, 77, 81, 87, 125, 134

fama, 70
Filson, John, 13, 43, 44–45, 52, 110
Finn, Huckleberry, 77–78, 94
Flint, Timothy, 13, 43, 46–47, 51

Gilkey, Richard Henry, 113, 127–32
Gilmore, Gary, 87, 94–97, 124
Gladney, Jack, 114–20, 127
guns/firearms. *See* violence

Hawthorne, Nathaniel, 108–9

Hephaestus, 17
Hemingway, Ernest, 14, 26, 47, 75, 76–85,
86, 92
Henry, Frederic, 78–79, 83, 84, 85, 86
Herodotus, 19
Hesiod, 19–20, 24, 28, 103
Hitler, Adolph, 113–14, 115
Holden, Judge, 3, 12, 15, 24, 38, 53, 58, 59,
73, 77, 87, 91, 98–111, 113
Homer, 12, 17–19, 21, 22, 33, 46, 58, 72, 90,
108, 140n4 (chap. 5)
Hume, Kathryn, 88
hyperautonomy, 5, 8, 13, 14, 15–16, 58,
67, 70, 71, 75, 77, 97, 99, 111, 112–32,
134–37

idiotes, 12, 24–25, 30, 31, 54, 56, 59–60, 61,
122, 128, 130, 136
individualism, 5, 6, 7–9, 60, 65, 101, 112

Jackson, Andrew, 52, 109
Jefferson, Thomas, 3, 5, 6, 13, 14, 15, 26, 27–
41, 42, 43, 45, 52, 54, 58, 61, 64, 66, 68, 69,
70, 83, 92, 115, 133–34, 135, 139n1 (chap.
2); Declaration of Independence, 2, 4, 11,
27, 28, 29, 31, 34, 35; "Nature's God," 2, 27,
29, 35, 36, 40, 51, 56, 60, 61, 62, 66, 68, 73,
79, 80, 92, 112, 134; *Notes on the State of
Virginia*, 2, 11, 32, 33–36, 40, 49, 103; "tree
of liberty," 36–37, 126, 135
Jehlen, Myra, 5, 6, 9, 35–36, 58, 101, 129

Keesey, Douglas, 121
Kelly, Barney Oswald, 87
Kennedy, John F., 120–22, 125, 128

lathe biosas, 26, 81
Lawrence, D. H., 13, 51, 52
Leclerc, Georges-Louis, Comte de Buffon, 33
Lee, Henry, 27
Lewis, R. W. B., 35; "American Adam," 5,
51, 92, 108
Lincoln, Abraham, 29, 135
Lindberg, Gary, 74

Madison, James, 27, 133
Marx, Karl, 21, 123
Marx, Leo, 27, 35, 45, 78
Mailer, Norman, 14, 26, 33, 35, 48, 59, 67,
75, 77, 85, 86–97, 99, 100, 106, 113–14,
115, 116, 120, 121, 122, 124, 125, 126;